learning
to
breathe
again

Selected lyrics in this volume have been recorded
on the following Tammy Trent CDs:

Set You Free
   "He's Right There" by Todd Collins and Lisa Kimmey
   "My Irreplaceable" by Michael Gavin, Ray St. James,
      Steve Siler, and Tammy Trent

You Have My Heart
   "Welcome Home" by John Mandeville
   "You Don't Have the Strength" by John Mandeville and
      Steve Siler

Breathing
   "Father God" and "New Life" by Tammy Trent and
      Pete Orta

For more information about Tammy Trent Ministries, visit:
www.tammytrent.com

learning
to
breathe
again

Choosing Life and Finding Hope after a Shattering Loss

tammy trent

W PUBLISHING GROUP™

www.wpublishinggroup.com

A Division of Thomas Nelson, Inc.
www.ThomasNelson.com

Published by W Publishing Group, a division of Thomas Nelson, Inc., P.O. Box 141000, Nashville, TN 37214.

Scripture quotations, unless otherwise indicated, are taken from the Holy Bible, New International Version. Copyright © 1973, 1978, 1984, International Bible Society. Used by permission of Zondervan Bible Publishers.

Other Scripture references are from the following sources:

The King James Version of the Bible (KJV).

The Message (MSG), © Eugene Petersen 1993, 1994, 1995, 1996, 2000, 2001, 2002. Used by permission of NavPress Publishing Group.

Song lyrics and other borrowed materials are used by permission of the copyright holders. Please see complete credits on page 213.

The stories in this volume are true, but in some instances, names and details have been changed to protect identities.

Library of Congress Cataloging-in-Publication Data

Trent, Tammy.
   Learning to breathe again : choosing life and finding hope after a shattering loss / Tammy Trent.
      p. cm.
   ISBN 0-8499-1826-X (hardcover)
   1. Trent, Tammy.   2. Lenderink, Trent—Death and burial.   3. Bereavement—Religious aspects—Christianity.   4. Christian biography—United States.
   I. Title.

BR1725.T665A3   2004
277.3'083'0922—dc22   2004005548

Printed in the United States of America
05 06 07 08 QW 9 8 7 6

*T*HIS BOOK is dedicated to the greatest love my heart has ever known here on earth.

Trent, through the memories of your undying love and faithfulness to me, I'm learning to breathe again, somehow, without you. I never got to say good-bye to you, and I will always hate that. So I hold on to the day when I will get to say hello again in heaven.

What is it like there, Trent? What are you doing? Each day that passes here brings me closer to the day I'll see you again. Don't forget me, Trent. I'll be there sooner than you think, and I promise we'll still be the best of friends.

Thank you for all you gave to me throughout my life. I will be forever changed because of who you are to me. I love you always.

—Tammy, your girl

contents

acknowledgments

I WOULD LIKE TO THANK THE ACADEMY . . . Wait! That's a different project. (smile) Here go the real acknowledgments.

To Jesus: Thank you for paying the ultimate price for Trent and me on Calvary so we would feel and know hope that can come only from you. Thank you for your presence and love and hope in my life. I do believe . . . even in the hard times.

To Mom and Dad: (That's the first time I can ever remember writing, "To Mom and Dad.") With my eyes filled with tears, I thank you both for loving me unconditionally. I've learned so much from your examples of Christ in my life. I love you both and the way you shine!

To my little sister, Gina: You are truly one of the most important people in my life. You've been my *big* sister so many times throughout this journey. I love you so much.

To my big brother, Norm: You have been the perfect picture of a big brother protecting his little sis. I love you, Norm, and the way you cry with me.

To Mom and Dad Lenderink: Thank you for loving me . . . especially now. I will always need you in my life. Of all the gifts you ever gave me, Trent was my favorite. Thank you for sharing him with me. He adored his family.

To Pam Thum, my very best friend: You've been there through it all, and you still love me. Your love and prayers for me have pushed away many dark clouds in my life. Thank you for your timeless friendship.

To my nieces and nephews, Joshua, Jordan, Anna, Amanda, Sarah, Jonathan, Kenny, and Kyle: You are always so quick to hug and kiss Auntie T when I'm sad. I love playing, snuggling, and hanging out with you all so much. All my heart, Aunt Tammy.

To Anita Rundell: I'm so happy the Lord brought you into my life three years ago. Who knew you'd become one of my best friends and traveling buddies? You've seen every side of me, and you're still here. Thank you for making me laugh again. I love you, girl.

To the Women of Faith team: Thank you for your healing love and acceptance that have been so gently wrapped around my heart these last couple of years. I love being with you and making you laugh! Now, put that thing away!

To Debbie Wickwire at W Publishing: You've always seen something special in this story and in me. I can never thank you enough for believing in and genuinely loving me. You're remarkable.

To Sue Ann Jones: Thank you for taking my words and then so beautifully bringing them to life through these pages. You will always be another angel in my life. What a privilege to work with you on this book. I felt completely safe.

To Lynn Morrow: Thanks for always looking out for me. You always seem to know my heart.

Thanks to Stephen, so unselfish; to Ken, so strong; to Diana, the perfect mom; to Keith, for loving my mom; and to Val, for loving my dad.

And to the countless friends, fans, and churches around the world who have prayed for me: I know I'm here today, pressing on, because you stood in the gap for me when I could not stand alone. Thank you, straight from the heart.

learning
to
breathe
again

Trent at the Blue Lagoon

prologue:
fifteen minutes

*A*FTER LUNCH we returned to the rental car so Trent could put on his diving suit. I waited while he sat on the car seat, his muscular, beautifully tanned legs stretching out through the door. He stuck one foot, then the other, into the legs of the stretchy, one-piece garment and stood up to pull it on. It fit his sleek, muscular body like a second skin, and once again I was reminded that I had married the world's handsomest man.

With the wet suit half on, he reached for my hand (that was our thing—we held hands everywhere we went) and walked together down to the dock alongside Jamaica's spectacular Blue Lagoon, where he planned to dive. On the dock, when his well-toned chest and six-pack abs were about to disappear behind the full-length zipper, I couldn't resist the urge to capture the moment.

"Trent, stop," I said, digging through my beach bag for the camera. "You look amazing. Let me take a picture of you right now. You look *great.*"

He shook his head good-naturedly, turned to focus his brilliant green eyes on the lens, and smiled that heart-melting smile I knew so well. I snapped the picture and returned his smile. He zipped up the dive suit, and we settled onto the edge of the dock's platform, swinging our feet in the clear, warm water. We were in a gorgeous place: the wide, shimmering pool of salt water varied from aquamarine on the edges to cobalt blue in the center of the 240-foot-deep hole. One side of the lagoon opened into a small channel that emptied into the Caribbean so that the blue-green transitions of the water seemed to blend into a sparkling mass of diamonds glistening on the sea. Around the lagoon was a jungle of luscious tropical foliage. It was one of the most beautiful places I'd ever seen.

Trent had been certified to scuba dive since he was twelve, and in the last year or so he had taught himself to free dive too, exploring deep water without an oxygen tank. As he did with everything new, he had done extensive research before he began free diving. He had read books, watched videos, and searched the Internet until he was totally familiar with the technique. Then he had practiced determinedly—in our bath-tub!—until he could hold his breath for five full minutes without emerging for air. Today he was eager to explore the Blue Lagoon without the bulky oxygen tank and regulator.

We sat there together a few more moments; we had done this dozens of times before during our eighteen years together. Trent loved to dive, and whenever we vacationed in a tropical place, he spent as much time as he could underwater. He would have loved it if I had dived with him, but it just wasn't for me. So I sat in my usual spot—beside Trent on the dock—as he pulled on his fins and got ready to go into the water. He adjusted his mask and snorkel, eased his underwater scooter over the side, then slid quietly into the water without a splash, as easily and smoothly as an otter.

He gently treaded water a moment as I gazed out over the glistening lagoon. Another dock—a swimming and sunbathing platform—floated near the center.

"Trent," I said, "do you think I could swim to that dock by myself and hold up a towel so I could lay out?"

He squinted in the sunshine, stretching his neck to look toward the dock. "You probably could, but I could just swim the towel over there for you. Here, let me have it."

"No, I can do it—don't you think?" I wanted the challenge, but still, it would be a bit of a swim, especially with one hand held out of the water.

He smiled at me. "Baby, I know you can do it, but I'll be back in fifteen minutes, so why don't you just wait, and I'll go with you."

"Oh, never mind," I said. "I'd probably get sunburned out there anyway. Then I couldn't lay out with you the rest of the afternoon, and I'd much rather do that."

Trent smiled at me, nodded, and turned back toward the lagoon. "OK. I'll be back in a little bit," he said. "Then we can do something *you* want to do. I'll see you in fifteen minutes."

"OK, Trent."

He pushed off, his body moving across the surface of the water as the little scooter pulled him toward the center of the lagoon. He kicked gently with the fins, his face in the water, as he glided away from me. I waited for him to stop, turn back, and wave, absolutely certain he would. That was another thing we did. We would say good-bye and walk away, then we'd turn and wave a little wave and leave again . . . and turn and wave a little wave and walk a bit farther . . . and turn again and wave. It was a standing joke with us, our silly repetitive waving.

And there it was. Trent stopped in the water, just at the point where the clear, aquamarine shallows shaded into the deeper blue. His face, encased in the mask, came up out of water, the snorkel protruding past his ear. He turned back to me, lifted his hand beside his head, and quickly bent his fingers forward and up, forward and up—the funny little wave I'd seen a million times in all sorts of places. His wide smile appeared beneath the mask. I smiled back at him, lifted my hand beside my ear, and mimicked his finger-flapping in the same tight little motion.

Then Trent turned toward the deep water, sank beneath the surface, and was gone.

1

Jehova Jira

Jehova Jira, my provider:
His grace is sufficient for me, for me, for me.
Jehova Jira, my provider:
His grace is sufficient for me.

And my God shall supply all my needs
According to His riches and glory.
He shall give His angels charge over me.
Jehova Jira careth for me, for me,
Jehova Jira careth for me.

—Merve and Merla Watson

1 The yummiest guy

1984

*E*VANGELIST DAVE ROEVER was sharing his riveting story that Sunday night in March at First Assembly of God Church in Grand Rapids, Michigan. So many people from all over the region had flocked to the church to hear him that an overflow room had to be set up. Being late, that's where my brother, Norm, and I ended up, sitting on folding chairs and watching the presentation on a large video screen.

A grenade had blown up in Mr. Roever's hand when he was a young soldier, permanently disfiguring him. His testimony described how his faith in God had helped him survive not only the injuries to his body but also the injuries to his mind and his emotions in the years since the accident. His story was fascinating. But I have trouble now, twenty years later, remembering many of the details of that remarkable night. Instead I was stuck in a mindless episode of teenage-girl silliness.

Before Norm and I left home that night, I stood in front of my closet and fretted that I didn't have anything to wear. I can close my eyes today and still see the outfit I ended up with: a funky green-and-brown sweater, a khaki skirt, cream-colored pantyhose, and some matronly brown pumps that used to be my mom's.

At the church, I settled in beside Norm on our folding chairs, and when, during the service, the pastor invited us to "greet one another," I turned around and found, standing behind me in the next row of folding chairs, the most gorgeous man I'd ever seen in my life. I think I even gasped at the sight of him as we automatically shook hands and said hello. *He is SO cute!* I thought, trying to keep my mouth from dropping open like a fish gasping for oxygen. And my next thought was, *Good Lord! Look what I'm wearing.*

"Hi, I'm Tammy," I managed to blurt out.

"I'm Trent," he answered, flashing the most spectacular smile in the whole state of Michigan.

He looked older, like a *man* rather than a fifteen-year-old, as I was that night. And he had a girl with him. *Probably his girlfriend,* I thought. *There goes* that *possibility.*

He definitely stood out from the crowd in his sharp, brown blazer that fell perfectly from his broad shoulders. Beneath the blazer he wore a soft, beige pullover and khaki slacks. He had a strong, movie-star jaw line, perfect blond hair, and a smile that exuded charm and charisma. I couldn't wait for the service to end so I could get another look at him. But when it was time to leave, he had vanished.

People had come from other churches all over the area to hear Mr. Roever, and since I hadn't seen the cute guy before, I assumed he was from another congregation. I felt sad, thinking I probably would never see him again.

A TRIO OF MR. UNIVERSES

A few nights later, I was back at church, sitting with some girlfriends near the front of the auditorium during youth group. First Assembly was a big, enthusiastic church, and that night, as usual, we were singing "Jehova Jira" seventy-seven times in a row (or at least it seemed like it) with our hands lifted high. I happened to turn my head toward the back just in time to see, walking in the door, the three yummiest guys I had ever seen. They were big, athletic, football-type hunks—and one of them was the guy I'd seen in the overflow room. *Trent.* I closed my eyes and silently shouted, *Thank you, Jesus!*

My heart pounded as the trio of Mr. Universes found a place to sit.

Then the coolest thing happened. Trent and the other two joined right in the singing of "Jehovah Jira" with their hands lifted up as they worshiped the Lord. There was something so absolutely attractive about that moment that I just knew I had to get to know them—and Trent was the one I had my eye on.

There were more than three hundred young people in First Assembly's youth group, so, to help the kids get acquainted, the big group would break up into fellowship groups based on the area of the city you lived in. Fortunately for me, Trent and I both lived on the north end of town.

I wanted to get to know this good-looking guy (probably like every girl in that youth group!), but when we met again in the small fellowship group, I lost my confidence as I got a closer look at what he was wearing. Trent had on all the cool labels: perfect designer clothes in the latest styles and best colors. He looked like the guy in Ralph Lauren's Polo ad. Sizing him up, I reconsidered my prospects, knowing that my family was obviously in a different income level. While we had everything we needed, we didn't have a lot of the things we wanted, including the coolest clothes. Thinking of my mom's hand-me-down shoes and the other plain, store-brand outfits that hung in my closet, I thought, *He'll never go for me. My family doesn't have the money to dress the way he does.*

Still, I wanted to give it a try. The fellowship group met at a private home, and the first time Trent attended, I poured on the charm. Suddenly I was Miss Sweetie Pie with the big servant's heart: "Can I get you anything? Would you like something to drink?" I was serving everyone, not just Trent and his brothers (the other two good-looking guys who had first appeared with him; the girl I'd seen with Trent the first night wasn't there). I finally sat down after taking around yet another plate of snacks, this one full of candy, and I was so excited, thinking, *We just shared some SweetTarts. Oh, I am SO going to kiss him later!*

Trent and his brothers were sweet but shy, and we probably hadn't exchanged more than a few words that night (including "Like some?" and "Thank you"), so I was shocked by what happened as the meeting ended. For some reason, I needed a ride home that evening; I can't remember why. But I spoke up as the meeting ended, asking if anyone could give me a ride, and as soon as the words were out of my mouth, Trent piped up. "We'll take you home," he said.

"You will? Awesome!" I practically shouted. Every head in the room turned to look at me, and every girl in the room was probably thinking, *You lucky thing!*

Trent didn't drive; I was surprised to learn that he wasn't old enough. Despite his mature, manly appearance, he was seven months younger than I was. In fact, while I was a fifteen-year-old sophomore in high school, he was a fifteen-year-old *freshman* at a different school. His older brothers, Tate and Troy, were with Trent that night, and one of them did the driving. Somehow (is it any surprise?) I managed things so that I just happened to end up in the backseat with Trent. Settling in beside him, I couldn't believe my good fortune.

"Was that your girlfriend with you the other night?" I asked, holding my breath, hoping he would answer the way I wanted him to.

"Hmmm. No, I don't have a girlfriend," he said, sending my heart into orbit. "That was Shelley. She lives with us."

I nodded sweetly, trying to sit still. What I wanted to do was jump out of the car and give someone somewhere a high-five.

Part of my wish came true. I did get to jump out of the car. Even though it was March, there was still snow on the ground (this *was* Michigan, after all). We were pulling away from the fellowship-meeting home when all of a sudden Tate shouted, "Snowball fight!"

Evidently among Trent and his brothers there was a frequent need for displays of rowdiness, and that was fine with me. I'd been a tomboy all my life, and I was sure I could hold my own in any snowball fight anywhere. So out we jumped, and the battle began. I was laughing so hard I could hardly straighten up to take aim at anyone, and my shoes were so slick that I spent more time sprawled in the snow than I did hurling snowballs. But I gave it my best shot.

BEGINNING THE ROMANTIC ADVENTURE OF A LIFETIME

I didn't have any gloves on, and by the time peace was declared and we had piled back into the car, my hands were nearly numb. I rubbed them together, trying to get the circulation going again. Without a word, Trent reached over and cupped my small hands in his larger ones; then he brought them to his lips and blew on them to warm them up.

My brain was racing with wild thoughts, especially one that blazed, *Oh, my gosh. If this guy didn't like me, I don't think he would do that!*

By the time the car stopped in front of my house and I trotted up the walk to the door, I was feeling lightheaded. On the porch step I turned to offer a little wave of my hand then ducked inside and fell back against the door, wondering, *What just happened? Is it possible he actually* likes *me?*

I could hardly wait until the next Wednesday night church service, hoping . . . well, hoping Trent would propose and we would live happily ever after. Instead, the second-best thing happened: he asked me to sit by him during the service. That's how this sweet love story began: two fifteen-year-old kids meeting at God's house and setting off on the romantic adventure of a lifetime. Trent was a young man who was driven by the things of God, yet he was so much fun, so full of life. It was very important to him, not only that we grow closer to each other, but also that we grow closer to God.

The first part of our "romance" was a bit complicated. I wasn't allowed to date until I was sixteen, so while I waited to turn sixteen I didn't date Trent Lenderink. I dated his whole family.

There were seven of them. Besides his parents, Tom and Sally Anne Lenderink, Trent had two older brothers and two younger sisters—plus assorted "adoptees." His godly family was forever bringing into their home a young person who had noplace else to go or who had family problems and needed a place to live until the difficult issues were resolved. The church would call them up and say, "Could you help this kid?" And for a couple of months or even a year, they accepted that young person into their home as family. Trent's mom told me later that she thought one of the things that influenced his life was that, as he was growing up, the Lenderinks always had people living with them. So the five kids grew up having to share their rooms, their beds, their belongings. It helped them all become more aware of others' hurts and needs. Mom Lenderink said she believed the Lenderink kids' love for and interest in others became a ministry to the people who passed through their lives.

The Lenderinks worked together in a group of innovative, family-owned businesses centered around wood products. Years earlier, Grandpa Lenderink—everyone called him Poppy—had started making specialty business cards from all kinds of wood, mostly as a hobby. He shaved the wood into slices about two-thousandth of an inch thick using machinery he had developed that would slice it, bake it, and print it. Soon the hobby turned into a major business that eventually was passed down to Trent's brother Tate, and the whole family worked together making, marketing, and shipping these products as well as several others.

The Lenderinks lived on property that was fondly referred to by outsiders as "the compound." The office and manufacturing facilities were located in the midst of hundreds of acres of family-owned forests. Their large home was nearby, nestled against a big lake, and Trent's grandparents lived on the property too.

The first time they brought me home with them, I eyed the jet ski stored in the boat dock, the four-wheelers, the trampoline, the dune buggy, the snowmobiles parked in one of the sheds, the beach volleyball pit beside the lake—all the "toys" and fun things anyone could imagine—and I thought, *Happy birthday to* me!

Our family dates usually followed this pattern: After Sunday night or Wednesday night church, Trent would ask me if I'd like to go with his family to Pizza Hut or Fables, another local hangout. "My parents will take you home afterward, OK?" he would say.

My heart in my throat, I hurried to ask my mom if I could go. I never wanted to ask my stepdad, Roger. He was usually the *no* guy. So I always went to Mom, and I held my breath, hoping she would say yes right away and not, "Go ask your dad," as she often did. Whenever she said I could go, I skipped back to Trent, the good news lighting up my face, and off we went. All eight of us.

The Lenderinks had an extended-version minivan. It was a white Caravan with the oh-so-cool simulated-wood paneling on the sides. I remember crawling into the car the first time we went to Pizza Hut and heading for the farthest seat in the back, hoping Trent would follow me back there. He did, of course. Then I sat there, my hands in my lap, hoping, hoping, hoping that his family would like me.

Trent was a sweet, polite young man, and I noticed right away that his family was protective of him. Actually they were all protective of each other. I didn't want to do or say anything that would give any of them a reason to think I wasn't the perfect girlfriend for their cherished son and brother! They obviously wanted the best for Trent—and I wanted to be that best.

THE FIRST KISS

The first night we went to Pizza Hut, I fell in love with his family. We laughed and joked and ate pizza until we couldn't hold one more slice of pepperoni. The outings became the highlight of my week. And then came the evening when, after feasting on pizza, Dad Lenderink pulled up in front of my house and said, "Trent, walk her to the door and give her a kiss."

I'm sure we both turned beet red! Especially when Trent's dad called to me, as we climbed out of the car, "Don't let him forget his manners, Tammy." Rolling his eyes, Trent walked me to the door, as usual, and with six pairs of eyes watching excitedly from the minivan, he gave me that first quick little kiss. It was nothing more than a brief tap of the lips, but it seemed to lift me right off the ground. I floated through the door and into my house then waltzed dreamily into my bedroom, thinking, *Oh, my gosh! I'm SO in love!* I pulled out a piece of paper and my box of felt-tipped markers and set to work creating a masterpiece of tribute to the guy who'd just stolen my heart.

"I Love Trent," I wrote in brilliant red marker on the white construction paper. Then I pulled out the orange marker and carefully outlined the first letters: "I Love Trent." Next the green marker came out: "I Love Trent." I had completely filled the entire sheet of paper with a rainbow rendering of my heart's passion when my brother walked into my room. He took one look at my artwork and sniffed. "You are so retarded," he said.

CAR DATES

I turned sixteen before Trent did, so I got my driver's license first. Not that it did me any good, because I didn't have a car. So Trent and one or both of his brothers would pick me up in the boys' big Jimmy SUV and take me out to the Lenderinks' home for our "dates." Then we would all pile back into the Jimmy, and they would take me home.

When I remember all the nights Troy and Tate waited in the truck, watching Trent walk me to the door and kiss me good-bye, I think it's a wonder they didn't die of nausea!

When Trent finally turned sixteen, he was away on a mission trip, so the driver's license had to wait. Even after he returned from the trip, there was no time to enroll in regular driver's ed and then take the test, because he was carrying a full load in high school and worked in the family business. But without my knowing it, he took weekly driver's ed classes at night for two or three months. Meanwhile Troy and Tate continued to be our constant dating companions and chauffeurs. It was tough for all of us.

Then one night, I opened the door and found Trent standing on the porch alone—and behind him, I could see that the Jimmy was empty. "Trent, you are going to get in so much trouble!" I scolded him. "I can't believe you're driving and you don't have your license."

"I know, I know," he admitted, always a little embarrassed that I was older than he was and had had my license for months already. He took me to a popular place called Robinette's about a mile from my house, and I thought, *OK, he's not gonna drive too far. Maybe it'll be OK.*

He disappeared inside the building and came out carrying donuts and cider. Then, as we sat there in the Jimmy, enjoying the treats, he reached into his back pocket, pulled out his wallet, and flipped it open, a huge grin plastered over his face. I turned the wallet so the light wouldn't glare on it and saw . . . his license.

"Trent! When did you get this? This is great! Why didn't you tell me?" I was so excited, thinking we could finally have a real "car date."

"I wanted to surprise you," he said, flashing that smile. It was the first of many years of sweet surprises. Trent loved to give me little gifts or cards, always unexpectedly. Out of the blue would come a little bunch of flowers or a card or something he had made from wood. I loved getting the gifts. But most of all, I loved being with Trent.

STAR-STRUCK

On one of our dates, Trent brought me to his house. It was the middle of winter, and he led me out to the shed where the snowmobiles were parked. He helped me into one of his sisters' snowsuits then lifted a helmet off the rack and set it gently onto my head. I watched through the plastic face shield as he pulled on a snowsuit and helmet himself. Then we climbed onto the snowmobile and took off.

The Lenderinks owned a lot of land. Much of it was forested and hilly, and we zoomed over the trails that night, loving the way the snow glistened in the moonlight. At the top of the biggest hill, Trent eased to a stop and switched off the key.

We sat there on the snowmobile, our helmets tilted back as we took in the vast expanse of stars twinkling in the cold, winter sky. In fact, I tilted my head back so far that, overbalanced by the huge helmet, I tumbled backward off the snowmobile, pulling Trent off with me! We laughed, sitting in the snow and enjoying the moment. And then Trent grew quiet and reached up a thick-gloved hand to touch my shoulder. We sat there, quietly staring into each other's eyes in the moonlight, looking like big-headed space aliens, and each of us thinking, *If I didn't have this darn helmet and snowsuit on . . .*

"We'd better go," Trent said suddenly.

"Yeah."

And the moment was gone. But summertime came, and the helmets stayed off, and the romantic moments continued. Sometimes I would come back home with the Lenderinks after an evening church service, and when everyone else got out of the van and went into the house, we *acted* like we were going into the house too. But instead, we sneaked back into the van to make out!

I loved kissing Trent. It was my favorite thing to do, and we did that every chance we got. I was so in love with Trent. This went on for four years, and as we gained physical maturity (and additional hormone surges) I wanted more. Our church's youth group was big on maintaining purity before marriage, and the "true-love-waits" message had been drilled into me since I was too young to even know what true love was waiting *for*. But despite this background, by the time Trent and I were eighteen or so, my spirit was longing to be strong, but my flesh was weak.

I might have given in if Trent had asked. But in every instance, Trent was the stronger one. Every single time. Isn't that amazing? On those nights when our lips were chapped from hours of kissing and our hearts were pounding and our bodies were pushing us toward the next step, Trent was the one who would push me back ever so gently and show restraint.

"Baby, you are such a gift from God to me," he would say. "God's got a plan for us together. And I know a big part of that plan is remaining pure in our minds and in our hearts. It's going to be worth the wait, girl. I promise you. It'll be worth the wait."

Trent was the one who would say, "Stop."

I was the one who would answer, "I can't take any more waiting! What's the big deal?"

"Trust me, girl. It *is* a big deal," Trent would say. "You'll be so happy we waited. Trust me."

But for me, because of my background, trust didn't come easy.

2

I know what I'm doing. I have it all planned out—plans to take care of you, not abandon you, plans to give you the future you hope for.

—Jeremiah 29:11 MSG

2 loving hearts, broken

1973

I CAN CLOSE MY EYES and still see the scene. My parents had gathered us kids around the kitchen table. Mom pulled me onto her lap and held me close, and my brother, Norm, was in the chair next to us, leaning against Mom's arm. Across the table, my little sister, Gina, was sitting on Dad's lap, his strong arms wrapped easily around her.

Dad was crying.

Many details of that moment are permanently engraved in my memory while others have faded away, perhaps too painful to be recalled. I can still remember running my tiny, little-girl's finger along the grain of the wooden table as my parents spoke to us. But only bits and pieces of the conversation remain in my mind: "It's not working out . . ." "Mommy and Daddy won't be living together anymore . . ."

They had been sweethearts in high school, where Mom, a cute, five-foot-three dishwater blonde, had been a cheerleader and Dad, a six-footer who was two years older, was the star basketball player. Dad was kind and sweet and oh, so funny. And he was as handsome as my mom was beautiful. They had big dreams. Dad was being considered by college scouts because of his athletic ability but opted for Davenport Business College instead. Mom wanted to go into missionary work,

15

perhaps combining her love for the Lord with her music abilities. She had been named Miss Red Flannel Queen in a beauty and talent contest in Michigan, and had an offer to study music in Europe.

Dad had graduated in 1965, and Mom had one more year of high school to go. That summer the United States was drafting young men into the military to serve in Vietnam, and Mom and Dad were scared. "We both felt very strongly that if he went to war he would never return," Mom said later. "So we went for a drive one night. We parked the car, and as I cried in his arms, we came up with a plan to keep him out of the army."

YOUNG LOVE

Married men weren't being drafted at that time, but single men were. So, in January 1966, in the middle of Mom's senior year in high school, they were married. Dad worked in a factory, and Mom continued with high school, graduating with honors in May 1966.

"We lived in a small house but were very happy," Mom told me. "That is, we were happy until Norm [my brother is named after my dad] got a second notice from the draft board stating that his status had changed and now all married men, except those who were fathers, were eligible to be called up."

Well! They decided the only thing to do was to start a family, and, as Mom says, "God must have thought it was a good idea, too, because the next month the baby was on the way and Norm got his deferment papers."

My brother was born in December 1966, and seventeen months later, I joined the family: Tammy Ranae Hill, named after a Sandra Dee character in one of Mom's favorite movies.

Their family was growing, and their love continued, but despite that love, Mom and Dad drifted apart. Dad worked nights and during the days was often hunting or fishing while Mom was home with the two kids. Thinking she needed to "do something" with her life, she enrolled in beauty school, training to be a hairstylist. She had no more than started when she learned she was pregnant again. My sister, Virginia—she's always been Gina to us—was born shortly after Mom graduated from beauty school at the top of her class. When Norm was five, I was three, and Gina was six weeks old, Mom went to work.

SEPARATIONS AND RESTORATIONS

Mom and Dad's marriage survived a total of seven years, despite several separations. Both of them had problems and temptations; it wasn't just one spouse's fault. But that didn't lessen the pain for us kids. Dad was on a hunting trip in Wyoming when Mom called him and asked for a divorce the first time. In shock, he jumped in the car and drove nineteen straight hours through the night, rushing home to plead his case; he knew he and Mom had problems, but he couldn't imagine living without his kids. We were his whole life.

They separated and then got back together several times. But eventually the problems became too great, and they gave up. They divorced when Gina was about fourteen months old.

Norm, Gina, and I adored our parents. We grew up knowing that they loved us devotedly and thoroughly and forever. That love didn't change. But our family life did. Mom, Gina, Norm, and I stayed on in our little house in Cedar Springs, Michigan, but now our time with Dad was limited mostly to weekends.

It's hard for a kid of divorce to say anything negative, because you know your parents are already hurt about what's happened, and you don't want to cause them more pain. On her own, Mom provided a warm, safe, comfortable home full of love for us. But there was a hole in our family, a Dad-sized hole, because our dad couldn't be there 24/7 anymore.

I was a shy kid, and I think the divorce somehow sent me deeper into myself. When I think of my earliest school years, I see a favorite pink jacket. I wore it every day in cool weather. I can see, in my memory, the doors opening for all the kids to go outside to play. Maybe we were kindergartners or first graders. All the kids would go rushing out, but instead of heading for the playground, I would walk along a wall. I would take off my pink jacket, fold it to sit down on, and sit there on my jacket, leaning against the wall, watching the other kids play, waiting until recess was done. Every day, every recess, for I don't know how long. Sitting against the wall, watching and waiting.

I wasn't sad. That was just my way of dealing with things. I have always thought of myself as a survivor, and maybe that's when that attitude began. I was going through a loss, and in my little-girl way, that's how I dealt with it.

SATURDAYS WITH DAD

The highlight of each week was when Dad would appear on Saturdays, knocking politely at the door. The three of us kids would rush to greet him, eager to know what wonderful plans he had for us that day. It was always something fun. Dad totally devoted himself to having a good time with us for that whole day. He was a zealous athlete, and often the day would include going to some kind of ball game he was playing in. In the trunk of his car there would be a cooler packed with white bread and bologna, a bottle of ketchup, and some kind of cheap orange soda pop. Other days he would take us to the lake, and we would splash and play all day.

Being with Dad was so much fun. It still is. He is a practical joker and always ready to share a laugh. When we were with Dad, his mission was simply to make sure we were having a good time. He's still that way today. Wherever Dad is, there's laughter. Looking back, I marvel that we never got in trouble during our days with Dad—never got spanked on Saturdays. (I'm sure because we were such angelic kids!)

And the other thing that never happened was that Mom and Dad didn't bad-mouth each other to us kids. I can never remember hearing either of them saying anything negative about the other. But I *can* remember hearing my mom say, "Your dad loves you kids" and having my dad say the same thing about my mother. They were careful to keep their private thoughts to themselves—even though they probably had negative things to say.

The only sad thing about Saturdays was that we weren't allowed to spend the night with Dad. At first he had an apartment that was too small for all of us. Then, being a handsome, fun-loving, single guy, he had a girlfriend, Valerie, and our mom didn't want to risk having kids there if the girlfriend happened to spend the night too. So our day with Dad would end, and he would bring us back home to Mom, walking us to the door and sending us inside with a hug. More times than not, he said good-bye with tears in his eyes. He told me later how much he had cherished the times when he had tucked us into bed with good-night kisses—and how much it hurt to think he would never be able to do that again.

NEW FAMILY, NEW NAME

Mom continued working as a hairstylist, and a beauty shop client introduced her to her son, Roger Buffum. Eventually they started dating. Norm, Gina, and I watched from a distance, wanting Mom to be happy. One night, according to family legend (as remembered by Gina), my brother, who was about nine years old then, called a "meeting" of us kids one night after we were supposed to be in bed. I would have been seven and Gina, four. So I can't help but smile, imagining us sitting there together so seriously, preparing to discuss something of great importance: Mom's future.

"Tammy, do you want Mom to marry Roger?" Norm probably asked.

I can see myself twisting my little fingers and shrugging my answer: "I don't know."

"Gina?"

"No," she said.

"Well, we want Mom to be happy, don't we?"

Our heads surely nodded.

"And if it will make her happy to marry Roger, then I think we should say it's OK with us," Norm would have said. "We'll just have to grin and bear it." We weren't happy about it, because we wanted our own daddy to live with us again. But we swallowed our fears and disappointments and agreed to Mom's decision.

And that, according to Gina, is "how it went down." Mom and Roger were married in March 1976. Norm, Gina, and I stood stiffly in our best Sunday clothes with the rest of the wedding party, silently watching Mom and Roger exchange their vows. Then everyone went to the church basement for the reception: cake, punch, and gift opening.

A thoughtful friend had brought a present for each of us kids too. Mine was a Holly Hobbie doll. Always a tomboy, I'd never had any interest in dolls, but I loved *that* doll. When Mom and Roger left for their honeymoon, I took it with me to Aunt Donie's house. My favorite aunt, Aunt Donie, was Mom's sister, and she took care of us kids while Mom and Roger were gone. Norm and Gina did just fine, but there I would be, every night of the honeymoon, tucked into the guest room bed in my pink-and-white polka-dot pajamas, hugging the Holly Hobbie doll, and crying for my mom. I felt sure Mom had a new life and was never coming back for me.

When Mom called, I tried to be brave, but the tears came anyway, and I asked, "Mommy, when are you coming home? Come home, Mommy!"

I suppose at that age I thought my mother had left forever and was never coming back. My dad was gone, and now my mom had left me too. Aunt Donie told me again and again, "It's OK, honey. Your mommy's coming back. You'll see." But I didn't really believe it until Mom told me herself.

Her voice coming through the telephone reassured me. "Tammy, Mommy loves you very much," she said. "I'm coming home in four days to get you."

"You are?" I said, feeling a morsel of hope. "OK, Mommy."

I can just imagine what it must have been like for Mom—trying to have a good time and enjoy a beautiful honeymoon with her new husband, while a tearful little girl on the other end of the phone line begged her to come home! Of course she and Roger did come back, and our life as a new family began.

One of the first things that happened was that we all took our stepdad's last name. Roger became "Dad," and our daddy became "Real Dad." To keep things straight here in the book, I'll keep calling them Dad and Roger, which is what I call them today. But as soon as Mom and Roger married and he moved into our home, Roger immediately became the one we called Dad. I consider these changes now and think how much it must have hurt our real dad—probably as it hurts millions of divorced fathers out there—to hear his kids call another man Dad.

Roger wanted to legally adopt us, but Dad wouldn't allow it. Still, we were unofficially given his name; we had no choice. No one said, "Do you want to be Tammy Hill or Tammy Buffum?" It was simply done. Roger said it would be better for us in school and that we would feel more like a family. So we became Norm, Tammy, and Gina Buffum.

That decision also caused our dad a lot of emotional pain. I know that now, but back then, the divisive issues were kept away from us kids, and that was probably for the best, because we certainly weren't prepared, as youngsters, to fight those battles. Still, I know now how much it hurt my sweet, adoring daddy to have his beloved kids called by another man's name. He even believed, or was led to believe, that later, when we were old enough, we had our last name legally changed to Buffum.

My brother, Norm, *did* have his name changed legally when he was eighteen. He loved Roger's father, who became our grandpa; Norm and Grandpa Buffum had a great relationship. So Norm changed his name, in part, to show his love for Grandpa. But there were practical reasons too. He had fallen in love with and proposed to a beautiful girl, Diana, who knew him as Norm Buffum and just assumed that after they married, she would take that name too. But, of course, that wasn't Norm's legal name, so it wouldn't be *her* legal name either unless he officially changed it.

Realizing how much of a problem it was going to be to get married, have a family, and launch a career while having two different names—a legal name and an assumed name—Norm knew that changing his name was really the only choice he could make.

Dad didn't learn of Norm's decision until, at the end of his wedding, the pastor introduced the couple as "Mr. and Mrs. Norm Buffum." Dad tried not to show the pain he felt, but Val let Mom know later that they were both hurt over it. After that, there was even greater distance between Mom and Dad.

Because it was something we just didn't talk about, Dad thought Gina and I had legally changed our names too. Somehow, just before I married Trent, the topic came up, and Dad mentioned that I wasn't going to be Tammy Buffum much longer. I said, "Dad, you do know, don't you, that I'm really Tammy Hill? Roger gave us kids the name

Buffum, but it's not a legal thing. I didn't change my name legally." I dug through my purse and pulled out my driver's license to show him.

If only I'd known the joy it would have brought him to clear up that misunderstanding, I would have done it years earlier! And now, here I was, telling him this great news just as my last name *was* going to change legally—to Lenderink. But my sweet, caring Daddy had never let us know how much the issue had hurt him. When he saw that name, Tammy Hill, on my driver's license, he was so happy, tears welled up in his eyes.

But all that happened much later. When Mom married Roger in 1976, the reality for us kids was that our name was now Buffum, and our day-in, day-out dad was Roger. Our name had changed, and now our world was about to change in a big way.

3

He's Right There

It's not hard to read you; it's so easy.
It's like I can read your mind.
In fact, the empty expression on your face,
It shows what's going on inside.
You've got lots of questions,
And the answer is just like it was before.
He is waiting on the sideline
When you realize you just can't take any more.

— Todd Collins &
Lisa Kimmey

3 | wishing for more

$\mathcal{F}$ROM A CHILD'S PERSPECTIVE, Roger and Dad were as different as two fathers could be. Dad had left when he and Mom divorced. In contrast, Roger was always there, always dependable, a good provider and definitely a leader. He took good care of us, and I must admit, he taught us discipline and respect.

Dad, on the other hand, was a fun-loving guy whose main goal in life was to show us a good time. When we were with Dad on those deliciously happy, laughter-filled Saturdays, we always had fun, fun, fun. Anywhere we went together, I could crawl up on Dad's lap and feel embraced not only by his arms but by his heart. We didn't have to work for Dad's love and affection. It was as steady and sure as the sun. He loved us wholeheartedly and playfully.

CRAVING FATHERLY AFFECTION

Roger struggled to find humor in anything. And although he *wanted* to love us, he just didn't know how. He especially didn't understand what it really meant to show love to a child. I wanted so much to crawl up onto Roger's lap and feel loved and cherished the way I did when I was with

25

my real dad. With Dad out of the picture except on Saturdays, I didn't get nearly enough of that kind of fatherly affection.

Looking back at those years, I admire and appreciate my mom more than ever. She loved us deeply and unconditionally, and she loved us for what was missing from our lives. Dad wasn't around daily to give us the love we craved, and Roger really didn't know how to love us in the way we needed. Although she didn't replace Dad, Mom loved us enough for all of them.

Still, she was limited in how much she could do to ease our day-to-day situation. She loved Roger, she respected him and wanted us to show respect to him, and she was a submissive wife following scriptural guidelines as best she knew how. In so many ways, Roger was a good man, but as a parent he was moody and emotionally detached. All we had known about fathers was from warm, funny, happy-go-lucky Dad. So it was a shock for us kids to realize that this man who at times could be cold and critical was going to be our father from now on.

A NEW DAD, A NEW HOME

Roger moved into our little house in Cedar Springs, but after a year, he moved us about an hour's drive away, to Grand Rapids. With Roger and Mom both working, we could afford to live in a subdivision we kids thought of as a "real" neighborhood, and we had more of the material things middle-class families can afford. I would have traded all the clothes and the bedroom of my own for a sign of tenderness from Roger. As a teenager I fought for his attention, hoping for affection. Sometimes I would buy him a card and write on it, "Dad, thank you for being part of my life. I love you. Tammy." I'd leave it out somewhere for him to find and then feel crushed as I peeked around a corner to see him open it, glance at the message, and set it aside, never mentioning it to me at all. It was almost as if I could see on his face that he wanted to love me but just didn't know how.

I don't mean to paint a picture of Roger as an ogre. He was probably doing the best job he knew to do as a father. But I also can't say our home was a happy place. I knew I was loved by my dad, but he wasn't there.

And I knew I was cherished by Mom, but she wasn't able to counter Roger's coldness.

The atmosphere within our family hinged on Roger's mood at that moment. When he came home from work and was in a good mood, we were overjoyed. At dinner we would laugh and joke and twitter with exciting reports of what had happened to us that day at school. But when Roger came home in a bad mood, it was as though a storm cloud hung over the house. We kept quiet and tried to stay out of his way.

After we moved to Grand Rapids, I made lots of friends at school, but we kids rarely had anyone come over to our house. We always preferred playing or hanging out at someone else's house. There the mood was light and happy. Our house was that way too, unless Roger was in one of his moods. We never knew if he would say something embarrassing to our friends—or act like we were the happiest family around.

DAD'S NEW FAMILY

Incredibly, Dad continued his policy of never saying anything negative about Roger. And he continued to see us regularly even though he now had a new family of his own to love and enjoy. He and Valerie were married, and now our Saturdays were spent at their house, where we happily became brother and sisters to Val's three kids, James, Becky, and Kenny.

While Dad was busy falling in love with Val, I developed my own crush on Val's son, James. Of course, it was an adolescent-type crush where you swing from building forts together one minute to giggling and sharing a silly little kiss inside the fort the next! But the interesting thing was that once Dad and Valerie were married, James and I never again held hands or kissed as boyfriend and girlfriend. Now we considered ourselves brother and sister, so that wouldn't be proper at all! Still, James is precious to me, and we have a warm and comfortable relationship.

All six of us kids were in Dad and Val's wedding. I loved Val, and I was glad to see Dad happily marrying her, but I did have a problem with the wedding. Being a tomboy, I detested having to wear a dress, and that's what I remember most about that day—how much I hated wearing that frilly dress. But as much as I hated the dress, I loved Val. She was—and still is—the coolest lady ever, and she absolutely loves us.

One winter weekend when we were at their house, the six of us kids built an eighteen-foot snowman. It was so spectacular, the newspaper came out and took pictures of us. And once again we were convinced that we had the best dad in the whole world.

Such memories help me remember that, even in our broken and blended family, I was blessed to feel loved by my mom, my dad, and Val. There was a big difference in Dad and Val's home and the home where we lived with Roger, and that difference saved my sanity. Val never made Norm, Gina, and me feel any different from her own three kids.

The interesting thing was that, financially and materially, Dad and his new family had less than we had living with Roger. They lived very simply while we had moved into middle-class status and had a few more toys and extras. But still, we loved being at their home. It was a place of laughter and love. Dad was a hunter, so we would often have venison and rabbit, and Val would make the most delicious homemade french fries.

That was how my life unfolded during that stage: great memories even in the midst of wishing my parents could have worked it out. On Saturday evenings when we left Dad and Val's house (even though they were married now, Roger still wouldn't let us spend the night with them), I always felt sad—and maybe just a little jealous of Val's kids, thinking, *Our dad is the best dad ever, and you get to have him all the time, but we don't.*

A CHURCH OF FAITH—AND FUN

Before the divorce, Mom had always taken us kids to church and Sunday school; Dad rarely went with us. Roger, on the other hand, took us to church and made sure we never missed.

At first we attended a church that only had one or two services a week. It was a simple, no-frills denomination where you showed up on Sunday, said some prayers, heard some Scripture verses, listened to the sermon, sang "God Be with You," and went home. Then, when I was thirteen, we visited the First Assembly of God in Grand Rapids and fell in love with the inspiring service and the enthusiastic attitude of the congregation. We came away thinking, *Wow! You can actually have fun in church!*

Mom and us kids were ecstatic, especially Mom. First Assembly reminded her of the spirit-filled Pentecostal church she had grown up in. So when we found First Assembly, Mom was in heaven. We anxiously held our breath, waiting for Roger to say it was OK for us to go there, and he did.

I quickly became best friends with the pastor's daughter, Tammy Benson, and she helped me get acquainted with members of the church's huge youth group and all the other activities it arranged for young people. Now church was Sunday morning, Sunday night, and Wednesday night, and the friends and fun I enjoyed there became my most common way of escaping the tension I felt when Roger was home.

Now that we kids were older, Mom had more time to devote to the ministry, something she had wanted to do for as long as I can remember. She began traveling around the area speaking and singing at Women's Aglow gatherings. And she became the women's director at First Assembly, a position she held for more than sixteen years.

The rest of us became very involved in church, as well. Roger and Mom would sing in little groups sponsored by the church, and Roger also ran the church's sound system every week. Norm and I played in the orchestra. He played trumpet (he's still a great trumpet player), and I taught myself to play the drums. I loved playing percussion, even when I was an itty-bitty girl, maybe as young as seven. Gina was involved in the children's choir and the church's musical dramas.

Church was a pleasure, the bedrock of my existence. But Roger managed to find ways to take the fun out of it. To him, church seemed to be more about rules than about Christ's love for us. And, as he saw it, he was the one who oversaw the rule book and decided if anyone had messed up.

4

My Father's Eyes

She's got her Father's eyes,
Her Father's eyes;
Eyes that find the good in things,
When good is not around;
Eyes that find the source of help,
When help just can't be found;
Eyes full of compassion,
Seeing every pain;
Knowing what you're going through
And feeling it the same.
Just like my Father's eyes,
My Father's eyes,
My Father's eyes,
Just like my Father's eyes.

—Gary Chapman

4 | sporty little drummer girl

*D*AD ALWAYS BELIEVED we kids could do anything we dreamed of doing. He was our biggest, most loyal supporter. On a Saturday shortly after the divorce, we were with him on another great weekend adventure, and the plan for the day was a get-together at a snowmobile club in Cedar Springs. A band was playing, and we were all having a good time. The next thing I knew, I was standing up there with the band playing a tambourine!

I was still a very little girl, maybe eight years old, but there I stood, shaking my head in time with the music, a huge smile on my face, and the tambourine going like crazy in my tiny hands. And right there on the front row, cheering me on, was Dad. I don't know exactly how I ended up playing with the band, but I'm sure he was the one who made it happen, coaxing and encouraging me, probably winking to the band members and pointing my way until I was standing up there in front of everyone, giving my first performance as "an artist."

I was thrilled. Afterward, I skipped out to the car, eager to tell Mom the big news when Dad dropped us off. But it was snowing heavily as Dad drove us home, and our car hit a patch of ice on an overpass and skidded into a guardrail. Gina hit her head on the dashboard, and when I saw the blood, I jumped out of the car and started running down the middle of the snow-covered road, screaming and crying. Poor Dad! Now he's got one bleeding child in the car and another one tearing off down the highway! I don't remember where Norm was, but I'm sure Dad was concerned about him too.

"Gina's OK!" Dad shouted as he hurried to catch up to me. "Wait, Tammy, it's OK. Everyone's OK. Your sister's OK." Somehow he managed to get me back in the car, make sure Gina's head had stopped bleeding, check on Norm, get the car back on the road, and deliver us back home. I promptly ran into the house, not to brag about my first performance as a rock star, but to wail, "Mom! Dad got us in a wreck!" It was not the best way to promote peace between my two recently divorced parents.

A few years later, when Mom and Roger were married, they traveled around presenting music programs in area churches. As Mom's reputation grew, she was asked to open for Christian recording stars like Larnelle Harris and Carman when they came to town. She was really the "star" of our family; Roger ran sound for her and sometimes he sang with her too. Often they brought us kids along. Sometimes Mom would take us when she went into nursing homes or other little places where she was invited, and we might sing with her occasionally.

FIRST STEPS TOWARD THE SPOTLIGHT

When I was nine, Mom asked me if I'd like to sing my first solo at one of her musical performances. It happened right after I had adopted Amy Grant as my very own special hero. Mom and I were on our way to the mall to go shopping—one of my favorite things to do, both then and now. I love being with my mom anytime, anywhere. But to go shopping with Mom at the mall, well, that was the best.

We were riding in the car, listening to an AM Christian radio station, and a song came on that just blew me away:

> Giggle. Giggle if you want to.
> But I know it's still true.
> That He's always gonna love me.

So just laugh out . . .
If you think I'm uncool,
Playin' the part of the fool,

'Cause I love Him!
Don't you know how I love Him?
Oh, well, I do!

"Mom, who is that?" I shrieked, nearly causing her to run off the road. I loved the song and couldn't wait to hear it again.

Mom said it was Amy Grant, and I begged her to take me to the music store the minute we got to the mall and buy the cassette for me (no CDs back then!). The album was named for the title track, "My Father's Eyes," and I absolutely loved it. Amy was a teenager then, probably fifteen or sixteen, and I was nine years old and head over heels in love with her music. It's a miracle I didn't wear out that tape, because I played it constantly. Every night I would fall asleep listening to it. Sometimes I would even cry because I wanted so much to meet this girl with the beautiful voice and tell her how her music had affected me.

My dream came true a short while later when my stepdad's sister, Terri Buffum, called out of the blue and said, "I bought tickets to see Amy Grant, and I want to take Tammy with me." Amy was performing at Calvin College in Grand Rapids, and I was absolutely thrilled that Aunt Terri was offering to take me. I drew a big red heart around the date on my calendar and X'ed off each day, counting down to the concert.

Our seats were way in the back, but I didn't care. I was nine years old, attending my first-ever Christian concert, and I was awestruck by all the cheering, clapping kids and especially by Amy, up there on the stage. I took it all in, trying to absorb every detail of what was unfolding before me, and I absolutely knew at that moment, *This is what I want to do. I want to do this someday.*

That really started everything for me. I began following Amy Grant's career faithfully, clipping out every magazine article and photograph I could find. I would even cut out her name wherever it appeared. I made a huge photo album with all the stuff I'd collected about Amy, and I went to her concerts and took my camera, snapping pictures of her during the performances. All my friends knew I was an Amy fan, so they would ask Christian bookstores for any Amy Grant displays they were finished with. Soon my whole room was converted into an Amy Grant shrine, covered floor to ceiling with Amy Grant posters and displays.

My parents—especially my mom—started getting concerned about me because she thought I was becoming obsessed with Amy Grant, and I guess I was. Although I would have to say, if that was true, Mom was my primary enabler! One Christmas, everything on my wish list was Amy Grant tapes. And in my stocking Christmas morning, there they were: eight or nine Amy Grant cassettes. However many albums she had at that time, I owned them all. By the following Christmas, Mom was trying to introduce me to other recording artists, and I liked some of them a lot. But in my mind, no one compared with Amy.

AMY'S MINE!

The funny part of the story concerns my little sister Gina, who's three years younger than I am. At those ages—I was heading into preadolescence and Gina was seven or eight—she always wanted to be everywhere I was and do everything I did. I loved Amy Grant, so Gina loved Amy Grant too. She wanted to be with me when I was with my friends. She wanted to be in my room. And I, being the impatient big sister, would say, "Gina, leave me alone." I was at that age when I just didn't want my little sister around. And I didn't want her copying everything I did.

Now Gina's one of my best friends, and I adore her. But I remember sitting down with her one afternoon and saying, "Gina, we have to talk. Amy Grant is *mine*. You need to find your own favorite."

Gina looked absolutely stricken, so I hurried on to say, "Look. I'll help you find someone else. We'll find someone for you together." I flipped open a *CCM* magazine, and together we went through the pages to find somebody. We came across this particular singer, and I told Gina, "Oh! She's for you. Her name is Michele Pillar, and she will be yours."

Gina was the little sister; I was the big sister. Obviously, I was the boss. So she said meekly, "OK." Then she started cutting out all the

Michele Pillar stuff she could find, and she pasted it in an album and hung pictures on the wall, until one day she came to me and said, "Tammy, I don't *like* Michele Pillar!"

Reluctantly, I agreed to share Amy Grant with Gina. But still, *I* was the biggest fan, and when Mom asked me if I'd like to do a solo at the family's next music program, I knew instantly what song I wanted to do: Amy's hit song, "Father's Eyes."

We were singing for a Methodist congregation in Grand Rapids. I can close my eyes today and see it in my memory, even today: a little church at Three-Mile Road and East Belt Line. I was very nervous, singing a solo for the first time in front of that mid-sized gathering. I feel the same way today, stepping onto a stage in front of an audience of thousands: nervous, but eager to do it. At that first performance, I was fortunate to have some special friends in the crowd: Grandma and Grandpa Buffum were there, sitting proudly near the front, their faces beaming with pride. They were amazing grandparents—a Christian couple who loved Norm, Gina, and me as though we were related to them by blood.

Mom had gotten me the performance track for "Father's Eyes"; that would be my accompaniment. My heart was pounding as I stepped to the front and reached for the microphone, but once the track began and I began singing, the nervousness left me, and I was so glad to get to sing that song!

I can't really remember what kind of reaction I got that night from the audience. Certainly, no one rushed down the aisle and tried to sign me up for *Star Search*. I'm guessing the response was more along the lines of, *Bless her heart. What a cutie.*

GAINING EXPERIENCE, BUILDING CONFIDENCE

When I got a little older, I competed in an Assemblies of God event called Teen Talent. One year, singing Kathy Troccoli's song "Stubborn Love," I went all the way to nationals in that program and earned a little trophy.

Gradually I was gaining experience and building confidence. Mom had been teaching me to love and appreciate music for a long time, and maybe she felt now that it was paying off. In my youngest days, she had sent me to my Aunt Margaret for piano lessons. How I hated them! At each lesson, Aunt Margaret would grimace, listening to me attempt the latest assignment. "Tammy, you didn't practice this week, right?" she would say.

"Right, I didn't practice," I would shamefully reply.

The truth was, I just wanted to play the drums. Maybe it was that early experience shaking the tambourine at the snowmobile club—or teaching myself to play percussion in the church orchestra. I have no idea where that love came from, but that was the music I loved most.

Then I hit fifth grade, and before the end of the year the middle school people came around and asked who was interested in being in the band the following year. They went down the line of volunteers, looking at us and asking, "What do you want to play?"

When it was my turn they asked me what I wanted to play, and I said, "I want to play the drums."

I can remember the teacher saying sympathetically, "Honey, you're just too tiny to play the drums. And besides, you're a girl. You can't play the drums."

"But I just want to play the drums," I whined.

She answered confidently, "You look like a flute player. You're gonna play the flute."

I shrugged and said OK, and the teacher handed me a paper to sign. Later, Mom and Roger bought me a flute, and in sixth grade, that's what I played. I stuck it out for two years, until the beginning of my eighth-grade year. Then I went to my band director and said, "Please, please, please! I want to play the drums! I don't want to play the flute. I want to be a drummer."

The band teacher said, "OK, I'll let you play the drums. But if you really want to do that, you're going to have to start with the sixth graders. You're an eighth grader, and you'll have to start over with the sixth graders. It's going to be very humbling for you, but if that's what you want to do, I'll let you try it."

"I'll do whatever I have to do," I told her. So the next week, there I was, an eighth grader, playing the drums with the sixth graders. She was right: It was a humbling experience. I felt so stupid. But in less than two months she moved me back up to the eighth-grade band. Then, in ninth grade and all through high school, I happily played percussion.

"LET BUFF DO IT!"

At my high school, Forest Hills Northern, we had an awesome band director, Paul Olley, and one of my favorite times to play was during the boys basketball games, when Mr. Olley would turn us loose with the latest pop music. He was very young, maybe just twenty-five, and he was very cool, very hip, and really into pop music. During class time, we would learn all the usual stuff, but during the last ten minutes he would lead us through current hits like "She's an Easy Lover" or "Celebrate Good Times, Come On!" or something by Lionel Richie or whoever was at the top of the charts. Oh, boy, we were jamming!

Mr. Olley was brilliant. He charted out what every instrument would do for every pop song. And that's the music we would play at the boys basketball games. Mr. Olley would take out his bass guitar and join us. Best of all, he would roll out a full drum kit. There were usually three of us drummers (the other two were guys), and we all took turns playing, rotating through the set. I will never forget playing on those wild and wonderful Friday nights. Of course all my peers and friends were always there. We had an awesome basketball team, so the gymnasium was usually packed. My nickname then was Buff, short for Buffum, and sometimes my friends would shout, "We want Buff! Let Buff play!"

Then, if it was my turn, Mr. Olley would give me the nod, and I would hop up to the drum set, settle myself coolly on the stool, and just go to town, playing "Celebrate" or some other loud, upbeat song. I remember thinking, halfway through one of those songs, *My arms are killing me!*

One time Mr. Olley called out, "Come on, Tammy! Keep up." And I was so embarrassed, thinking, *I can't do this!* But, surprisingly, I didn't feel insecure. I thought, *I'm a girl, and I'm probably not going to be as good as those two guys, but I can hold my own, and everybody likes to see the fun I'm having.*

It was such a shock when Mr. Olley died. In my junior year in high school, he was diagnosed with cancer. He ended up in the hospital, and because I worried that he might not be a Christian, I wrote him a letter. I had a friend who was going to the hospital to see him, and he took the letter. In it I told Mr. Olley how much he meant to me, what an awesome teacher he was. For one of the Assemblies of God Teen Talent competitions one year, I had asked him to take Amy Grant's song "Ageless Medley" and transpose it for me, and he did the whole thing, just by listening to the cassette: guitar, drums, bass—everything. He was so talented. I took what he had done and ended up singing the song with a live band for the competition. In my letter to Mr. Olley, I thanked him for always giving of himself to me and to everybody.

Then I asked him to accept Jesus as his Lord and Savior because I knew he wasn't going to make it many more days, so I was begging him. "What have you got to lose?" I asked him. "If it's not true, it's no big deal. But if it *is* true . . ."

As a kid, I was doing what I could to persuade him: "Just please, please, please, do this, Mr. Olley . . ."

My friend took my letter to him, and he died a day later. So I don't know if he was able to read the letter. I don't know if he accepted Jesus. It was traumatic to me to lose someone who meant so much to me and not know if he knew the Lord. What I'm hoping is that I'll meet Mr. Olley again in heaven. Maybe I'll find him by following the sound of that cool bass guitar.

MY SPORT OF CHOICE

Music had become important to me. But it wasn't as important as sports. Always the tomboy, always following my dad's lead, I was into sports big time, and basketball was my sport of choice. I started playing in ninth grade. My high school had three girls teams: freshmen, junior varsity, and varsity. So in ninth grade, I started playing with the freshmen. After about two weeks, the coaches came to me and said, "We want to move you up to varsity."

I said, "You've got to be kidding me!" As flattering as it was to be asked, I really wasn't excited about making the move. On the freshmen girls team, I played the entire game; I never sat the bench. I sometimes scored thirty points a game! I loved it. My dad, a real pro at the sport, had taught me a lot of his techniques. In addition to his skill, I had his genes, so there was probably some natural ability there.

When I played with the freshmen girls, I'd watch them dribble the ball and think, *Good grief! Anyone could just steal that from her—so OK, I will!*

It was easy for me. But when the coaches said they wanted to move me up, it bothered me because I thought if they switched me to varsity, I'd spend most of my time sitting the bench. So, to their astonishment, I said no.

Then we went through a couple more games, and the varsity coach came back to me and said, "Look. You don't have a choice. We're moving you up. We need you up there."

My strength was mostly in ball handling. In fact, I think I may still hold the record for steals and assists in my high school. I was short, but I was very fast, and the coach told me he needed my speed. So I moved to varsity, and immediately I started the game.

Here I was, a ninth grader, a little tyke, playing with and against the big senior girls from all these different schools. I played varsity all four years. At about the same time I was moved to varsity as a freshman, the coaches also moved up my good friend, Lori Bennett, who was also a freshman. She was tall and played center. We loved the game, loved playing varsity, but we also felt bad, because now we had friends who were sidelined because we had moved into their positions.

One of them was Lisa Verbrugge, a senior, who now was sitting the bench while I started in her place. It bothered me a lot to cause her any disappointment. She was my friend, it was her last year, and now she was benched because of me. Even while I loved playing every game, I hated seeing Lisa sitting there on the bench. But despite that awkward situation, we became even closer as friends.

That summer, between my freshman and sophomore years, Lisa died. She was a camp counselor, and she and her campers were doing some kind of variety show when she just fell over, dead. Perhaps it was an aneurysm, but she was just a young girl, so whatever it was, it made no sense at all.

I was stunned by Lisa's death. I was one of those girls in high school—and so was Lisa—who wrote notes all the time. We passed them throughout the day—during class, in between classes, as we passed in the hall, stuck in the vents of lockers. We were the queens of note passing! I had shoeboxes full of notes from my friends. After Lisa died, I found all my notes from her and read them again, remembering all the fun times we'd had. That was the first loss I went through. I couldn't know then that, years later, I would be tearfully rereading other notes from someone else I had lost.

THE GIFT OF MUSIC

During high school, sports became my favorite activity, but music was a strong second. I loved music, a gift I learned from my mom. She ministered with her music, not only in churches and women's groups, but in our home. Some of my sweetest memories are of those times when I would be sick, miserably feverish and achy all over, and Mom would sit at my bedside, stroking my hair and softly singing to me. I can close my eyes, feel her hand gently pushing my hair off my face, and hear her singing, in that soft, sweet, soprano voice, "Softly and tenderly, Jesus is calling. Calling for you and for me . . ."

Mom also used her music to entertain people, and I love doing that too. I think it's something I got from both my parents. While Mom is the singer, my dad is totally an entertainer; he'll do anything to get a laugh. And it is completely how my brother, sister, and I are today. Norm, especially, is a fun-loving guy, just like Dad. He's the one who watches a funny movie and keeps rewinding it to the funniest spot over and over and over until someone says, "Norm, for heaven's sake! Stop!"

As a teenager, when I wasn't playing basketball, I was performing with the high school band or playing in the church orchestra or singing in the First Assembly youth group or appearing with my mom at churches and nursing homes and other gatherings. And sometimes I presented little programs on my own: "Oh, you're Judy Buffum's daughter? Would you come sing for us?" That kind of thing. I would pack up a big boom box and a microphone, along with the performance-track tapes that would provide the accompaniment, and off I would go to churches or nursing homes. Sometimes I sang at banquets or other events at Christian schools. Watching my mom, I learned at an early age how to perform all by myself.

As Mom's reputation spread, she and Roger organized different bands over the years that would perform Christian music. For a while they performed with a guitar player and a drummer, and Mom played the keyboard and sang.

The little band practiced for an hour or two every week in our house. We lived in a big neighborhood, and on practice night the windows in our house would be wide open while Mom and Roger, with the guitar player and the drummer, jammed away. People walking by would stop and peer inside.

THE PHANTOM DRUMMER

The memorable thing about this particular band—and almost my downfall—was that the drummer had an awesome drum set, and he left it at our house in between practice sessions. I remember coming home from school and walking closer and closer to that drum set. I checked out every piece, every inch of it, fascinated by its components.

Finally, knowing I was playing with fire but unable to resist the temptation, I settled onto the stool and gingerly picked up the drumsticks. Ever so lightly, I rapped one stick against the head of the snare drum. I closed my eyes, imagining what it would be like to abandon all caution and launch into a hard and fast rift.

I sat there, thinking about the possibility, knowing if Roger came home early and caught me messing with the drums I would probably be grounded for weeks. But I simply couldn't resist. I turned on Roger's stereo—something else we kids were absolutely forbidden to touch, but I knew how to turn it on. I picked out some music I liked—maybe something by Russ Taft or Amy Grant, Kathy Troccoli or Sandi Patty—

and I slid back onto the drummer's stool and jammed to the music. I loved it!

Fortunately, I never got caught, but I shudder to think what would have happened if Roger had caught me messing with his stereo and playing someone else's drums! But the allure was just too great; the urge was too strong. I'd sit there for the longest time, playing those drums and picturing myself as the coolest rock star in history; I would play until my brother or sister's warnings finally sank in—"Tammy, you're gonna get in so much trouble!"—or until they yelled, "Stop it! You're driving us crazy."

When I thought it was about time for Mom or Roger to come home, I would turn off the stereo and make sure everything was in exactly—*exactly*—the same place it had been. Then I was out of there, the phantom drummer, disappearing into thin air.

Christian music and basketball were my lifelines during those busy teenage years. They kept me happy, active, and out of the house. Basketball brought praise and excitement. Music brought me closer to God.

Then along came Trent.

5

For one of our very first dates, we went to Trent's house and made pizzas. I showed off my incredible cooking ability by opening the can of Chef Boyardee sauce. Trent was hooked.

5 | moving on

WHEN I TURNED SIXTEEN and was allowed to date, Trent and I often shared double or triple dates with his brothers; the four or six of us packed ourselves into the family's minivan or in the boys' big Jimmy, which was jacked up so high we girls needed help climbing in. Later Tate and Troy started dating two of my best friends, Michelle Ferris and Tammy Benson, and that was the best thing imaginable. The six of us hung out together constantly, and whenever we were together, there was always lots and lots of laughter.

Amazingly, the place the six of us ended up most frequently was the Lenderinks' home. There was so much to do there—the snowmobiles, the jet ski, and the beautiful acreage to explore. Plus, they had a huge house, and we kids loved nothing more than to gather there to watch a movie together or to play some kind of game or listen to music. The Lenderink boys always had a plan for something fun to do. And they showered us girls with cute little gifts and flowers. I'm sure that was their mother's influence on them. She's such a devoted mom and thoughtful woman. Valentine's Day, Easter, birthdays, Memorial Day, Fourth of July—whatever the holiday, there was Trent with a little gift for me: some flowers or candy or a little trinket of some kind.

I even got gifts on the holidays nobody ever heard of. Knowing Mom

Lenderink so well now, I can just imagine her looking at her calendar and saying, "Trent, Tuesday is Sweetest Day. You need to get Tammy a card. Write her a little note, and surprise her with it."

And I can imagine him then, a teenage boy, saying, "Come on, Mom! I've gotta get her a card for *that*? Nobody's even heard of Sweetest Day!"

It was probably a pain for him to do as a teenage guy. But how grateful I became for his mom's gentle influence on Trent's life. He became the kindest, most thoughtful young man any girl could ever dream of. And today some of my most cherished treasures are the notes and cards Trent gave me over the years (or hid for me in places where he knew I would find them). There are dozens of them, all signed with his chicken-scratch handwriting, and each one brings the deepest memories.

Tammy, Michelle, and I sometimes entered little singing competitions around the area, and the guys would come along and bring us flowers after we performed and did our thing.

A GOOD TIME OF MY LIFE

While Trent and I attended different high schools, we still managed to see each other at church, and we had a "real" date once a week. That was all Roger would allow. I had to pick a Friday or Saturday to go out with Trent; Roger wouldn't allow me to do something with him both nights, not even go to his house with a bunch of other kids. Another rule was that I could not call Trent on the telephone; Roger didn't believe girls should call boys, so Trent always had to call me.

Despite these rigid rules, it was a good time for me. I was blessed to have the world's cutest, most thoughtful guy as my boyfriend plus a wonderful group of friends from school and youth group. I had music, I had basketball, and I had a mom, a dad, and a stepmom who loved me completely. Plus I had a stepdad who, while not the warmest and kindest father figure, provided stability and everything I needed materially and loved me the best he could.

High school flew by, and graduation day came. I wasn't all that sure what I wanted to do next. Trent and I had dated steadily for more than two years, even though we had had little breakups here and there. They were always my doing, stupid little teenager spats when I would say, "I don't like you today. I'm breaking up with you for a week." One time we broke up for a month, but I think we both knew these little breakups weren't serious. Actually, I can't imagine why Trent didn't get fed up with this kind of silly behavior on my part. It just shows again that he was always the mature one, the steady one. Despite these little moments of teenage crisis, I assumed Trent and I would probably get married eventually. But first I just wanted to explore life a little. And somehow, I wanted to sing.

COLLEGE BOUND

Still nurturing that seed of an idea that had swept over me at that first Amy Grant concert, I secretly dreamed of being a recording artist. *What a cool thing, to think of myself as an artist,* I thought. I had done a couple of recordings in a private studio in Grand Rapids, and I had made a little video and other amateur things, but they were mostly just for myself. Nothing ever came of them. What I really wanted to do was make a professional demo tape and send it out to the record companies. But coming right out of high school, I just didn't have the resources, the contacts, or the knowledge to make that happen.

My friend Tammy Benson was planning to attend Bible college in Florida, and she told me, "Tammy, you've got to come too!" But I was reluctant. All summer Tammy tempted me with colorful descriptions of the fun we would have attending college together. I applied for admission and was accepted, but I still wasn't sure I wanted to go. Finally Tammy said to me, "Tammy, it's in *Florida.* We live in *Michigan.* What are you thinking? You've gotta come!"

Finally, about a week before Tammy was to leave, I agreed to go. Somehow, right from the beginning, I knew I would be gone just one year. I thought, *I'll have this experience, then I'll come back home.* I also thought it might be good for Trent and me to have some time apart, just to make sure we were absolutely right for each other. Of course I was sad to leave him, but I had never been the type of girl to say, "I can't live without you."

Instead, I told myself, *I can do this.* I had survived other challenges in my life, and I knew I could survive this one. And besides that, I knew it was going to be fun, an adventure. I thought, *I'm going to do this so I can say I experienced college. I'll make some new friends, and maybe after a year I'll know what I'm supposed to do with my life. But if I don't, that's OK too. I'm just going to enjoy life and take it one day at a time.*

Trent, on the other hand, was watching me go and thinking, *I could lose her.*

Mom, Roger, and Tammy's parents moved Tammy and me to Florida. My parents gave me a food card, so my breakfast, lunch, and dinner were paid for every day, but otherwise I had no car, very little cash, and no job. During high school breaks I had sometimes helped Trent's family in their business, so I had a little money saved up from that.

Mom and Roger said, "We love you. Bye." And I was on my own.

Trent—always my sweet, thoughtful Trent—would send me gifts in the mail: big boxes of cookies, chewing gum, and other treats. And he sent flowers. Sometimes he would tuck a twenty-dollar bill in a card and send it to me.

Then, early in the first semester, he said, "Tammy, I've got an 800 number—our office does. So if you need to call me, just use that toll-free number." Wow! What an awesome thing. I used that 800 number and called Trent day and night. I also called all my other friends back home—until the day when Dad Lenderink saw the office phone bill and asked, "What *are* all these phone calls?"

Trent took the fall for me; that's the kind of guy he was. He didn't say, "I told her she could use it to call *me.* I didn't say anything about calling half the population of Michigan!" Instead, he said, "Dad, I'm sorry. That's my fault. I gave her the number and told her she could use it." Then he called me and said, "Tammy, you're getting me in trouble!"

Classes started in August, and while I was enjoying college, by October I was eager to come home for fall break. I found a ride back to Grand Rapids with a guy and his sister who were driving through the night. It was a Sunday morning when I got home. I hadn't told my parents I was coming, so when I rang the doorbell, Mom opened the door, saw me standing there, and burst into tears—and so did I.

I hadn't told Trent I was coming, either. So I hurriedly changed my clothes and went with my family to church. His sister spotted me first, and I pulled her aside so we could work out some details. Somehow we managed to time things just right so that Trent was standing there, waiting for the elevator, and when the doors opened, "Surprise!" There I stood, inside the elevator. The happy look on his face was worth the twenty-four-hour drive.

We had the best time that week. Trent and his brother Troy were always buying old sportscars and fixing them up to sell. At that time he had a fun little Ferrari, and we zipped all over the place, enjoying the spectacular colors of Michigan in the fall, and loving our time together. Kissing Trent after two months apart was the most marvelous thing. I couldn't get enough of him. In fact, I wanted more; I might have *given* more. But even though I was the "smart" college kid, and Trent was still in high school, *he* continued to be the one who demonstrated maturity every single time.

"Wait, Tammy," he would say. "We've gotta wait. I want God's best for you, and we both know that means we have to wait." It touched my heart that Trent would place my well-being over both our physical desires. *What a guy,* I remember thinking, amazed at his integrity and self-control.

BREAKING UP

The week passed like the blink of an eye, and soon I was back in school. Thanksgiving came and went, and finally, in December, I went home for semester break.

The first thing I did when I got back home was to break up with Trent.

Back at Bible college in Florida, I had met some guys who were much more like me than Trent was. They sang, they wanted to be in ministry, and they played basketball. Trent couldn't sing at all, had no plans to go into the ministry, and he played every sport *but* basketball. It felt like I had so much in common with these other guys, I couldn't help but consider that, since I wanted to sing someday, wouldn't it be perfect if I married someone who did too?

There was one guy who especially interested me. I'll call him Jeremy. He had a great voice, and, like Trent, he was incredibly good-looking and seemed interested in me. Jeremy's dad was a pastor, and I had this image of Jeremy and me going into ministry together. Maybe he would be a pastor, and I would sing . . .

So I came home for Christmas, thinking, *Well, I've gotta know if this other thing is what I'm supposed to do.* So, without any real reason that Trent could understand, I came home and broke up with him.

He cried when I told him. We sat there together in his living room, and tears rolled silently down his cheeks as he asked, "Why, Tammy? Why are you doing this? Is there somebody else?"

It was difficult—and the next three weeks of Christmas vacation didn't get any easier. Sometimes when couples break up, they turn the hurt into something mean or spiteful. Trent was never like that; he never said anything harsh to me, never accused me of playing games with him, when probably that's what I was doing. When we spotted each other at church during Christmas vacation, I would act like it was no big deal; I was careful to maintain an I-don't-miss-you attitude.

Trent, on the other hand, never played that game. He missed me, and anyone with eyes saw it on his face. At church I might be over here talking to a group of friends and he'd be over there talking to a group of friends, and he'd look my way and oh, the hurt I'd see in his eyes. He didn't act like I did: *I'm with my buddies, and it's OK. I don't miss you.* No, Trent was too honest for that. Sometimes he would just look past his buddies and smile at me. Other times mouth the words, *Tammy, I miss you.*

Early one morning while I was home a noise outside my window woke me up. It was Trent, pecking on the glass. I opened the window, and he said softly, "Tammy, are you sure? Could we just go out Friday, just to a movie or something? Could we just do that?"

I said, "Trent, no, we can't."

He nodded his head with a little smile and said so sweetly. "OK. I'm sorry—sorry to bother you, Tammy."

The hardest part of the breakup came at Trent's high school Christmas prom. I had been booked to sing at the prom with my friend Steve. He and I did a lot of singing together; Steve was a neat guy who liked me and wanted to date, but I just wanted to be friends. It always bothered Trent a little bit to see me sing with Steve; I think he wished that he and I could sing together. But that was never going to happen because Trent couldn't sing at all. He was tone deaf. As they say, he couldn't carry a tune in a bucket.

So there I was, broken up with Trent and booked to sing with Steve at Trent's prom. The event was held on a boat, and while there wasn't really anything you could call dancing—this was a conservative Christian school—there was really great music (provided by *moi*, as Miss Piggy would say) and lots of fun. Trent was going to be there, and even though I probably denied it, I was bothered, thinking about seeing him with another girl.

Steve and I were up on stage doing our music when Trent walked in—and he had not *one* girl but *two* with him! Later I learned that it had caused a ruckus in the school because some people were saying, "That's not fair. He's taking two girls. He needs to just take one." Trent was one of the most popular guys in the school, a leader in student government and a sports star, so I used to tease him that it was probably some of the mothers who got mad, complaining that Trent wasn't taking *their* daughter to the prom. I can imagine them saying, "If he can take *two* girls, why not *six*?"

Later I asked him, "So what's the deal? Why two girls?"

He told me, "Tammy, when you came onto the boat to sing, I didn't want you to see me with one girl and think I was dating her. I figured if you saw me with two girls, you would know there was no possible way I would date both of them at the same time. You would know I was taking them both as friends."

That was Trent: kind, thoughtful, and caring. Even after I had hurt him as I did, he was determined not to do anything that would cause *me* hurt in response.

A NEW BOYFRIEND

When I came back to school after Christmas break, I told Jeremy I had broken up with Trent, and he was happy. We saw each other frequently during the next couple of weeks. Jeremy's family lived in Tampa, and Jeremy asked me to drive there with him on Friday night because he wanted to help some friends move from an apartment into a house on Saturday. My roommate was dating Jeremy's best friend, and the four of us went together. The plan was that we would spend the night with Jeremy's parents, then the guys would help with the move the next day.

We got to Tampa late Friday night to find that his parents were not home; in fact, they were gone for the whole weekend. We sat around talking and listening to music in their house for a while, then, very awkwardly, we agreed it was time for bed.

While Todd and Lori were carrying in our backpacks, Jeremy led me to a room and said, "You and Lori will sleep here, and Todd and I will be in the other room."

I said OK and smiled good night. But the whole thing made me very nervous. I didn't like it, being alone in this house, just the four of us, and having no way to leave and not knowing anyone nearby to call in case problems arose. But I went ahead and got ready for bed, thinking Lori and I would simply have to trust the two guys. After all, we were all Christians, right? We were Bible college students, for heaven's sake. If I wasn't safe in an environment like that, where would anyone be safe?

(Are you shaking your head as you read this, wondering, *What were you thinking!?*)

I had just gotten into bed when the door opened, and I assumed it was Lori, coming to bed. Instead it was Jeremy. "You know what?" he said guiltily. "It looks like I'm going to have to sleep in here, because Lori's in there with Todd, and the door's shut."

"Oh! Well, OK I guess," I answered nervously. I tried to act cool, but my heart was pounding. I was scared. Really scared. I'd been dating Trent for nearly three years, I was still in love with him and still a virgin, and now I was in this situation with a guy I liked but didn't love, and I was afraid of what would happen. It was such an awful experience. I lay there next to Jeremy agonizing over the mess I'd gotten myself into.

Except for Trent, I'd always been the no-strings-attached girl. We had both gone out a few times with other people, but I could kiss other guys at the end of the night and then say, "See ya!" I never wanted to commit to anyone. Trent was the exception, but by breaking up with him, I probably felt again that I was showing my independence, proving I could survive on my own.

Some have told me that attitude may have resulted from my parents' divorce and my father's leaving when I was so little. Or it may have come from trying to make Roger love me as a father would love a daughter and never being able to make that connection. After those kinds of losses, I was always careful not to get in a position where anybody could hurt me or disappoint me or leave me. And now that whole mind-set had led me to this place where I was lying in bed (fully clothed!) next to a guy I really didn't know that well, and I just felt sick—sick and scared—because I didn't know how I could get out of that situation. Worse, I knew I had no one to blame but myself.

Lying there next to Jeremy, my heart pounding and my fears racing through my mind, I thought of Trent. I had always felt safe with him, completely safe. I knew, beyond a shadow of a doubt, that he really loved me and cared about me, that he would never do anything that wasn't God's best for me. With Jeremy, I didn't know any of that!

The scene is so deeply etched in my memory that I even remember what I wore that night: sweatpants and a long blue shirt that went down nearly to my knees. Jeremy kissed me and made a few gestures to go further, but I said, "I'm sorry. I can't. I just can't." I was so relieved when he said he understood. Finally we both fell asleep.

The next morning, he left with Todd to help his friend move. Lori came into my room on the verge of tears. "I'm so sorry, Tammy!" she said. "I'm so sorry I did that to you last night."

I said, "OK, Lori, but don't do it again tonight." The deal was, we would be there both Friday and Saturday nights, and since I didn't have a car or any way to get back to school, I was stuck there. I said, "Lori, promise me you will *not* let that happen again tonight."

She said, "I promise you. I'm so sorry. I really let you down."

But that night, the same thing happened. She was locked in the other bedroom with Todd, so here came Jeremy, back to my room. Once again, nothing happened, but I felt sick about the whole experience, and when we got back to campus, Jeremy and I totally went separate ways. I think he was unhappy with me because we didn't have sex; I imagine him thinking, *I don't want to date this girl.* And basically I felt the same way.

We had enjoyed an awesome friendship, but that changed during the weekend. I remember lying there in the dark bedroom next to Jeremy, fuming, *I've waited this long to be with Trent, and you expect to walk in here and have me give up my virginity, just like that? I would be an idiot! If I were to give it to anybody before marriage, it would be to Trent, and I'm not even doing* that.

I was furious the whole thing had happened. Furious at Jeremy and, most of all, furious at myself.

Jeremy and I didn't even speak to each other the rest of the second semester. I didn't really date anybody. I had a bunch of friends, including guy friends. We would go out to dinner and do other fun things. I even kissed a few of them, but there was never any attachment or commitment.

THE OLD ELEVATOR TRICK

Back in Grand Rapids for spring break, it was inevitable that I would see Trent at church. He attended the Christian school that shared the church's property, so he knew the building well. Obviously inspired by my elevator trick back in October, he somehow managed to "accidentally" be alone in the elevator with me at the Sunday service.

I smiled. He smiled. The elevator doors closed and up we went. When the car was between the first and second floors, Trent pushed a button to stop it. Then, to my astonishment, he pushed another button, and the elevator's doors opened between floors. There was nothing there but a concrete wall. I was dumbfounded.

He smiled a mischievous smile as he turned toward me. I backed into the corner. "So," he purred like Mr. Smooth, "would you like to kiss me?"

"Nooooooooooo," I answered, an identical, teasing smile plastered across my face.

The next thing I knew, we were kissing and kissing and kissing. It never occurred to me that someone else might want to use the elevator! All I knew was that I was back in Trent's arms, and everything was normal again.

Finally we parted, and he said, "OK, so we're going out Friday?"

"Yeah," I said. And that was that.

Later we used to laugh, thinking about that time in our lives. We would say, "Yeah, we broke up for a while, and we never did officially get back together. All we know is, now we're married!"

6

My Everything

Your peace showers over me,
Your love so comforting,
Jesus, you are my everything.

Your strength I'm holding on
Your joy keeps me going strong
Jesus, you are the life I breathe.

I hear your rain falling down.
I feel your presence all around.

—Tammy Trent & Pete Orta

6 | love song

MAYBE YOU'RE EXPECTING ME TO SAY that I came home after that first year of college and married Trent. But that's not what happened. I came home from college and continued *dating* Trent. Both of us still had some growing up to do—and we had other things we wanted to pursue as well. We still assumed we would get married . . . *someday*. To reinforce that thought, when I came home from college, I went to work in one of the Lenderinks' businesses.

The whole family was involved in these businesses, and it was fun to be a part of what was going on. Trent's dad is a brilliant entrepreneur, and he has developed a wide range of operations dealing with wood products. The Lenderink companies produce the wood components for skateboards, they make drumsticks, and they produce veneering and plywood, among other things. The Lenderink property is a bustling place, and Mom and Dad Lenderink, all five of their kids, and the kids who were living with them temporarily would all have jobs there. Poppy Lenderink, who started the whole thing, still worked in the office then as well.

So it seemed like a natural thing, as someone who intended to be in the family someday, for me to work in the family business. One season I was a salesgirl, selling wood products made at the Lenderinks' mill in Wisconsin. Different die-cutting companies would call to order wood "dieboards" that they would use to make all kinds of products. In that job, I learned about the different kinds of wood, how they looked and what they could be used for.

The Lenderinks also have a Christmas tree farm; they started it as a hobby, another thing all the kids helped with, even when they were little. Eventually it grew into a major part of their business as they pruned, harvested, and shipped trees across the country. At Christmastime, they opened the farm for customers who wanted to cut their own tree. At first that was just another little sideline operation, but through the years, part of my job, with Dad Lenderink's guidance, was to help build it up, promote it on the radio, and turn it into an event with thousands of people coming out on the weekends. We served hot chocolate and offered free hay rides and a bonfire for the customers. It was a beautiful time filled with fun and hard work. I loved it.

Trent enrolled in college in Grand Rapids after high school; he lived at home and worked in the business during his spare time.

GROWING UP

In the summer of 1989, I took a leave from the family business and decided to join the Celebrant Singers, a ministry group that operated out of California. Once you were accepted into the program, you raised money to pay your own way for the summer. Then you went to the ministry headquarters in Visalia, California, where you were assigned to a team of singers and musicians. Most teams had about ten singers and twelve musicians, and they put you on a bus and sent you around to a different church every single night: Baptist, Lutheran, Catholic, Nazarene, Assembly of God, Methodist. Basically any kind of Christian church you can think of, we appeared there, singing our hearts out. My team traveled around the United States that summer, but we also went to Iceland. Another team went to Egypt, and a third team went to Alaska.

Celebrant Singers was, and still is, a wonderful opportunity for aspiring singers; the experience taught me a lot about ministry, travel, and music. And it taught me about serving others. Everyone on the team had a job to do, from unpacking and packing up the sound equipment to selling merchandise. I had what I considered the "poopiest" job: rolling up the microphone cords at the end of the night. I kept whining, "Could I not get a cooler job than winding these cords around my elbow?" But no, that was my job, and I became an expert at rolling up those cords.

I missed Trent terribly but still felt that it was good to be apart and to get this great experience. Things were different now between us. Trent knew he had nothing to worry about; he had started believing, *She does love me.* And he had also seen that I was growing up, becoming more mature; I was changing inside.

He started noticing that I was serving *him* more. It sounds so self-centered and ridiculous now, remembering our early times together. At first Trent was the one who was focused on serving; he did everything he could to make me happy, frequently surprising me with those little cards and gifts and special plans. I was mostly the taker at that point, not the giver.

Now, thanks to being with the Celebrant Singers (and, no doubt, a bit of growing up on my part) I was learning to give. And Trent, bless his heart, noticed even the littlest gestures. For example, one time when we went to the lake so he could go snorkeling, I waited on the dock for him, and when he came back, as he was walking to the car, I stepped up ahead of him and put a towel on his car seat so he could sit down without getting the seat wet.

Now, wasn't that a simple, common-sense thing to do? But I might not have done it before, might not have made that thoughtful little gesture. In fact, I might have even paused a minute before my own car door for Trent to open it for me. And he would have done it.

But now Trent was noticing that I was doing little kindnesses for him. He had talked to me, very gently, about how, as followers of Jesus, we need to develop a servant's heart. So that day, as I smoothed out the towel on his seat and stood back to smile at him, he said, "That was so sweet of you, Tammy. I love that in you. See how you're thinking of other people first? I can see a change in you." Then he added, "It makes me really happy."

You see, Trent loved me, but just as I had been looking for the right guy to marry, he wanted to marry the right girl. And he wanted his wife to have a servant's heart. He knew there was a little vein of selfishness in me. Not that he ever criticized me. But we would talk about what it meant to be Christlike, and I started changing. And he felt reassured, thinking, *This is the kind of woman I want to be with.*

READY FOR THE NEXT STEP

When the summer tour ended with the Celebrant Singers in autumn 1989, Trent and I knew we were ready for marriage. We looked at our finances and talked to our parents. I think it was a relief to them to know that, after all this time, we were finally going to get married. Trent's dad was especially glad because he was thinking, *If these guys don't get married, someone's gonna get pregnant!* He was probably right. We were twenty-one, we had dated more than seven years, and toward the end there, our times of intimacy were getting very, very close to the breaking point.

Sometimes I would drive myself to Trent's house late at night to see him, and we would end up snuggling on his bed. We would fall asleep together, just like that, and his mom would come in and say, "Tammy!" Or she would wake up Trent and say, "Get her out of your bed!"

Now, girls, I don't recommend this kind of behavior. It's fun, but it's way too tempting. And as I've said earlier, if it hadn't been for Trent's maturity and self-control, I'm not sure we would have waited to have sex until we were married. But oh, how glad we both were that we did. We wanted to be with each other all the time, and we just about were!

In fact, I lived at the Lenderinks' house for a short time. One night when I came home ten or fifteen minutes late from a date with Trent, Roger was waiting for me. He said, "If you miss curfew one more time, you are out of the house."

It was so frustrating for me. I thought, *Here I am, twenty-one, and I'm a good kid. I don't drink. I don't smoke. I'm dating a wonderful Christian guy. I'm a few minutes late, and you're going to kick me out of the house?*

Well, of course it happened again, and sure enough, Roger said to me, "You're out of here. You're out of this house."

The next day I packed up my things, got a girlfriend to share an apartment with me, and moved out.

I'm not even sure my mom realized what had been happening up to that point; I don't think she was aware of all the resentment Roger and I felt toward each other. By that time, she was distracted by the problems she was having with Roger, herself.

My new roommate and I barely had enough money to survive. In fact, we were so poor we somehow made it through the month of December without ever turning the heat on (not an easy thing to do in Michigan!) because we didn't have money to pay the bill. We only had a couple of pieces of furniture; I didn't even have a bed, just a mattress Trent had found for me someplace. A lot of the time, Trent would insist that I come home with him and sleep in a spare bedroom.

THE BIG SURPRISES

One night Trent picked me up and took me to a movie. When the movie ended, Trent said, "I'd like a hamburger. You wanna go to McDonald's?" I said sure. Because it was late, only the drive-through was open. So we pulled up and Trent talked into the speaker, ordering a couple of cheeseburgers for himself. Then he turned to me and said, "How about a Happy Meal, Tammy? You want me to get you a Happy Meal?"

I said, "That sounds good; I like the smaller portions. So yeah, get me a Happy Meal."

We pulled up to the first window, where you pay, and all these girls were coming up from the back of McDonald's, looking through the window at Trent and giggling and waving. I sat there watching how they were behaving, and I got mad.

"That's so rude," I fumed. "They're flirting with you, and I'm sitting right here beside you." Even worse, Trent was flirting back, smiling and winking at the McDonald's girls. It seemed to take forever to pay and get his change, and I was getting really disgusted. If we had a video of that night, you could probably see steam coming out my ears!

Finally we left the giggling girls and pulled up to the second window.

Another girl reached out to hand the stuff to Trent, and she was giggling and smiling just like the others! I was furious!

As Trent pulled away from the window he handed me the bag containing the Happy Meal. But by now I had completely lost my appetite. "No, I don't want it," I barked at him.

"Baby, open it up," he said.

"Trent, I don't want it. I'm not hungry anymore." I wouldn't even look at him.

He said sweetly, "Come on, Tammy."

But I wasn't having any of it. "Trent, I'm serious," I snarled. "I don't want it. Forget it."

He stopped the car right in the middle of an intersection (thank goodness it was late enough that there was no traffic!). He dug into the bag, pulled out the Happy Meal box, then opened it up and took something out. It was a little square box. A ring box.

"Open it," he said, his eyes twinkling merrily.

And there was the gorgeous diamond engagement ring. We had picked it out together a few weeks before but agreed that Trent would decide when the time was right to give it to me. Seeing it sparkle under the streetlights, I started crying. Trent started laughing. I felt so stupid for having been such a jerk. The McDonald's girls had been gawking and giggling at Trent because they were in on the secret, knowing we were about to get engaged.

The McDonald's manager went to our church, and she had held the ring for Trent and helped him work out the details. So they all were there, smiling and giggling at Trent—and probably wondering why he would want to get engaged to such a grump! Once the ring was slipped onto my finger, we drove to show Trent's grandparents, who were always known, not as Grandma and Grandpa, but as Goggy and Poppy Lenderink. Even though it was late, that's where we headed, and—no surprise—they were expecting us!

As if seven years of dating weren't enough, we had an eight-month engagement! August 18 was a date the church had available. It was also Gina's birthday, and she would be my maid of honor—one of *eight* bridesmaids in attendance. I hadn't really intended to have that many, but I just got carried away as I shared the news of my engagement with my girlfriends. A few of these girls hadn't been really close to me since we graduated from high school, and I hadn't actually planned on asking them to be bridesmaids, but when I told them I was getting married, they were so excited that I felt kind of bad. And before I knew it, I blurted out, "And I want *you* to be in the wedding!" Then I would have to go to Trent and say, "Honey, you've gotta find another guy to be a groomsman . . ."

One day that summer, Trent and I were out running errands, and he saw a yogurt place he wanted to try. I should have known what was coming, but as you may have figured out by now, sometimes I'm not the brightest bulb in the chandelier when it comes to anticipating surprises.

We sat down at a table, and Trent immediately popped back up and said, "I forgot something in the car." In a minute he was back, carrying a book, one of those magnetic-page photo albums. On the front, it said, "A Celebration to Remember."

He set it on the table and said, "Open it."

"Trent, what is this?"

"Just open it."

The first page was a beautiful tropical photograph, and above it, I read, "Hawaii Honeymoon, 1990."

"Oh, my gosh, Trent! We're going to . . . you're taking me to . . . our honeymoon is going to be in *Hawaii?*"

Trent knew I had always dreamed of going to Hawaii. I love anything Hawaiian. In fact, our wedding would have a Hawaiian theme. So he planned an awesome Hawaiian honeymoon for us (with his mom's help, I'm sure) and put together a whole book of photos, brochures, and itineraries showing what we would do each step of the way. And he chose a special place to give it to me: a yogurt shop named—what else?—Hawaiian Delight.

Trent led me through the book page by page: "OK, honey, our first night together, we'll be at the Radisson in Detroit. After the reception we'll fly from Grand Rapids to Detroit so we don't have to get up too early for the next day's flight."

He turned the page. "And look at this: Here are your luggage tags."

I rubbed my finger over the name on the tags: Tammy Ranae Lenderink. "Oh, Trent! This is awesome!"

But he was just getting started. Remember, Trent was a guy who *loved* to research whatever new thing he was doing. So he obviously had spent hours and hours studying and choosing all the things that would be fun to do on our honeymoon. Oahu, Maui, then the big island, Trent had gone all out.

"Trent, we're not just going to Hawaii, but we're going to *three* different islands there? Oh, my gosh!"

Each page had a photo or a brochure of the hotel or the airplane or the boat or whatever activity we would do while we were there. Even more surprising, Trent had bought a time-share condo! He had researched all the options and decided that, as much as it would cost to rent a condo or stay in a hotel for a week, or whatever it was, we might as well buy a time-share. "It's something we can enjoy for the rest of our lives, Tammy," he explained.

Once he had made that decision he had (of course) researched all the time-share options and found the most spectacular one at the most economical price. That was so much like Trent!

The book showed pictures of where he wanted to take me snorkeling, and, he said, if I didn't mind, maybe he would do some scuba diving. He had budgeted out how much money we could spend each day and planned for every possibility.

Then, on the last page, labeled "Homeward Bound," he had included a sweet little poem from a greeting card. My heart melted. I was so in love with this man!

WEDDING DAY

The big day finally came and, wearing a beautiful wedding gown borrowed from a friend, I walked down the aisle to become Mrs. Trent Lenderink.

You'll probably be surprised to read that *Roger* walked me down that aisle.

It's hard now, especially in light of all that would happen later, to explain why I chose Roger, instead of Dad, to walk me down the aisle. I can only offer my thoughts that affected that decision. Despite Roger's emotional distance, he had been the day-in, day-out father I had known for nearly twenty years. He was the one I called Dad. There had been some difficult times, but there were also some good moments, some very good memories. I had tried repeatedly during my younger years to reach out to him and connect with him as father and daughter. Maybe I thought this was one final gesture in that direction. I loved Roger. I wanted to have a father-daughter relationship with somebody, and while I knew my real dad loved me completely, because of the circumstances, he just wasn't around. So I asked the man who *had* provided for me all those years, who *had* been around.

Dad and Valerie were at the wedding, of course, and I know it probably hurt Dad to see Roger standing in his place. Yet I think he understood that the choices he and Mom had made in their lives affected many things, and this was one of the consequences. And, of course, Dad would never bring up the topic or complain about it in any way. Still, looking back on it today, I would have made a different choice, knowing what I know now.

There were eight hundred guests at the wedding, and at the reception afterward (continuing the tropical Hawaiian theme), we had a little water fountain inside a grass hut. People could go in there and have their picture taken. We didn't have a big sit-down dinner (who could have afforded *that* for eight hundred people?), but we served fancy appetizers and finger foods. And to top it off, a friend of ours who's an Elvis impersonator showed up in his Elvis costume to entertain the crowd. It was so much fun!

Afterward, our two families and closest friends went across the street to Mom and Roger's condo, and we had a nice, quiet dinner there and enjoyed a very comfortable time as a family. I laugh now, thinking about that afternoon in Mom's condo. Now we were married, and Trent and I were going to change out of our wedding outfits into our traveling clothes. I went into my brother's bedroom and said, "Come on, Trent. Let's change."

But he said, "I don't think I should be here." Instead, he went downstairs to Mom and Roger's bedroom and changed clothes there. Trent was always so careful not to offend anyone or to do anything that would put us in a bad light. That afternoon, even though we were married, he just said, "It's too soon, everybody's here, and it feels weird. I'm going downstairs."

Considering how long we had waited to take that next intimate step, and knowing how eagerly we were looking forward to it, it's probably a good thing we didn't change clothes in the same room that day. If we had, more than likely, we would have missed our flight!

7

Welcome Home

I was taken back when You took me in
Just to wipe my tears away.
You made no demands, chose not to blame,
Though I knew You had the right to.
And I saw the years I wasted,
Searching everywhere in vain,
Finding nothing to believe in until I finally
    heard You say:

Welcome home, My mercy's waiting.
Welcome home to open arms.
There's no shame in your returning
Though you may have wandered far.
Welcome home.

That was years ago, so far away,
At an altar on my knees.
But I can still recall like yesterday
How Your love forever changed me.
Oh, I see how You've been faithful
Though I've often caused You pain
And I've learned You won't forsake me
When I need to hear You say . . .

—John Mandeville

7 | making the break

RUE LOVE HAD WAITED, and now, after seven and a half years, the wait was finally over. Alone together that first night at the hotel in Detroit, we could finally enjoy the complete, physical love we had both been longing for all those years.

Throughout our dating time, Trent and I had believed that God's best for us was to wait until we were married to have sex. After we were married and my musical career got going, that was the message I shared from the platform every chance I got, especially when I was performing for young audiences. "True love waits" was more than just a slogan for us; it was reality. We had waited, and I encourage others to do the same.

The honeymoon was spectacular, and soon we were back in Michigan settling down to begin our life together. A new mobile-home park had opened just a half-mile or so from the Lenderinks, and Trent and I moved into one of the homes there. It was the coolest little place, mainly because it was *our* place. Trent built on a deck for me so I could lie out in the sun on summer weekends. And he built a gazebo.

He'd never built anything like that before, but he did his research—got books and videos and called a friend who was a builder—and one Saturday he and his friend just went out there and built that thing for me.

Trent was frugal with his money. He would never just go out and buy something major. He would research it. Then, when he had found what he wanted, he might look in the newspaper and see if he could find one somewhere else for a better price. To be honest, it used to drive me crazy sometimes. I would be in a hurry for whatever it was, and I would want him to make a snap decision and just go buy the thing. But that wasn't Trent's way. He always did his research, and that research always paid off.

During the four years we lived in the mobile home, we both worked for the Lenderink businesses, plus Trent went to school part-time to finish his degree. We were together day and night, and *one* of us had more trouble than the other focusing on the work at hand. It was just way too tempting for me to be so close to Trent and not be, well, *closer*. I was always sneaking back to his work area and trying to kiss him. (Girls, I am not kidding; *nobody* could kiss like Trent!) He would tolerate my silliness as long as he could, then he would send me back to my job. Trent was very motivated, strongly disciplined, and totally focused. When he was in there working for his family, he didn't mess around. No one ever had to tell Trent, "Hey, get back to work." His family had taught him well; they're all extremely hard workers.

Trent finished a junior college degree, then, after a break, he decided to go back to school to get a four-year degree. This time he enrolled at Michigan State in Lansing, about an hour's drive away. We would get up early in the morning, and many times I would drive him to school so he could sleep on the way. More than likely he had been up late the night before studying, and his class was at about 7:30. While he was in class, it would be my turn to nap; I would wait for him in the car, then, when his class was over one of us would drive back and we would go to work together.

MOVING INTO MUSIC

I worked in the family's business with Trent for eight years, and all the time I was working there, I was still dreaming of a career in music. I had recorded a few things here and there, just for myself, really, or maybe cassettes to sell when I went somewhere to perform. Mostly I had covered Amy Grant songs; I'd never recorded my own original music.

My best friend, Pam Thum, a recording artist who is like a big sister to me—we've been friends for more than twenty years—is also a gifted songwriter, and she has lots of connections in the music industry. She introduced me to John Mandeville, a record producer and also a great songwriter. One day I summoned up my courage and called him. "John, I would love to do a demo tape with you—maybe just three songs," I told him. "How much would it cost me?"

He said, "We can do it for two thousand dollars." Trent agreed that I should give it a try, and I flew to Nashville, went into the studio with John, and recorded three songs: "Someone 2 Love," "Hear My Heart," and "Love's Not So Far Away."

I mailed the demo tape to record companies all over the country, and nothing came of it. But I wasn't ready to give up. Pam and her friend Greg Long introduced me to another important contact: a very young, up-and-coming producer known as Tedd T, who was based in Minneapolis.

So, once again, I called and asked, "Could we do a demo tape together? And if we can, how much will it cost?"

This time the price tag was ten thousand dollars, but this demo tape would have the three original songs, in a remixed version, plus three additional songs—all original music—and a photo shoot. So we did the new tape, and again I mailed out dozens of copies. This time I had more contacts in the industry, thanks primarily to Pam. By then she had a record deal with Benson, one of the biggest labels in Nashville, and I traveled with her quite a bit when she attended industry events. I even went overseas with her a few times. I made a lot of friends on those trips; some of the people I met were in the music industry, and some of them were songwriters.

When the new demo tape was ready, I sent it out to these friends in the industry as well as to the record companies. Some were returned to me without being listened to at all. Once again, nothing happened. Then, after a couple of months, a record company contacted me and said its executives wanted to come see me perform. They did, but nothing happened. Evidently they didn't like what they saw, or else they didn't feel it would work.

At that time I was doing music that was very pop, almost hip-hop. Nobody was doing that in the Christian music recording industry. It was the style of Janet Jackson and Paula Abdul, and Christian artists just weren't doing it. That may have been why my phone didn't ring. And then, about six months later, the phone *did* ring. It was someone at a small label called REX Music in Nashville.

REX was small, but it had some great distribution. The executives decided to take the six songs on my demo tape, do a little tweaking, and add four more songs to create an album. REX released it in 1995, but before they did, the label executives called me back and said, "Would you consider changing your name?"

"What?" I asked. "What do you mean?"

I had sent in the demo tape under the name Tammy Buffum, and the execs asked me to consider changing my professional name to something a little catchier. I sat there in the mobile home, running through the possibilities. I liked the idea of taking a man's name as my last name, so my list of possibilities included names like Tammy Brice, Tammy Todd, Tammy Keith. Then suddenly I thought, *What about Tammy Trent?*

I called Trent, explained about the record executives' request, and asked, "Trent, what if I took your *first* name as my *last* name and became Tammy Trent?"

He said, "Gee, baby, I don't know. If you want to do it, I think that's great."

So that's how my self-titled album, *Tammy Trent*, was released.

What an exciting time. Imagine what it's like to turn on the radio and hear yourself singing! Actually, I noticed that I was hearing myself quite a bit. My dream of becoming a recording artist had come true. Even better, six weeks later, "Your Love Is 4 Always," the first single off the album that REX sent out to radio stations across the country, went number one on Christian hit radio, the youth-oriented segment of the industry known as CHR.

I was deliriously happy; the success of the record told me I was right where I was supposed to be musically. This was who I was, and I didn't have to change anything. I had finally found a label brave enough (and small enough) to say, "We want to take a chance on you."

Then the next song was released, and it became a top-five hit. The third song became a top-ten hit. It was all happening on the youth-oriented CHR, and I was thrilled. Now, if only I could break into an additional segment of Christian radio, the adult contemporary (AC) market. Those stations weren't playing my music at all, perhaps because I was too funky for them.

Just as this was happening, Trent and I had started building a home on the Lenderinks' property. Part of the foundation had been poured when the deal with REX Music happened. We knew, going into the contract, that REX didn't have a lot of money for promotion. We were going to have to spend some money on promotion too, and basically it came down to which we wanted more: to build a new home or to promote my music career. My selfless Trent didn't even hesitate. He said, "Baby, we've got lots of time to build a house. Let's wait awhile."

The problem was, we had already sold our mobile home and everything in it except our bed. We hated the idea of moving into an apartment and paying rent. But what else could we do?

It shouldn't be a surprise what happened next. Trent's generous and thoughtful parents said, "Why don't you just come and live with us?" They had that big home on the lake, and they were accustomed to having "displaced" people live with them temporarily when they were referred by the church. As a matter of fact, my friend Pam Thum was living with them at that time—not that she was displaced, but she was a family friend, and she was traveling so much on music tours that it was a big waste for her to rent an apartment. Realizing Pam's situation, the Lenderinks told Pam, as they had told so many people so many times, "Just stay with us. When you're home you've got a place to live; you don't have to pay rent."

It was a generous offer, and Trent and I were grateful. Still, as almost any wife (or husband) can tell you, living with your in-laws isn't the thing you want most. So I said yes, thank you, to the Lenderinks, and to Trent I said, "Promise me it'll be just a little while. We'll live with your family a few months, and then we'll figure out what we're gonna do, OK?" He said sure.

We were there five years.

It wasn't the ideal situation, but in so many ways living with Trent's parents was exactly the right thing for us at that time. We lived there rent free, all our meals were prepared for us, my best friend was there when she wasn't on the road, and when I took off to do my own road tours, Trent had his family to keep him company.

A couple of years later, the Lenderinks expanded their home to about six thousand square feet to include an addition that would serve as an efficiency apartment for Mom Lenderink's elderly parents, whom we called Granddad and MomMom, and for Poppy's sister—we knew her as Aunt Charlotte. Poppy had died a few years earlier, but Goggy still lived in their home next door, so it was like having our own little family village!

Trent and I lived upstairs in a large bedroom. We created a sitting and TV area that was sort of separate from the sleeping area. We had a private master bathroom, and there was a big walk-in closet. It was very nice, very comfortable, and we actually had a lot of freedom and privacy whenever we wanted it. I was totally spoiled, living there. The family's offices were right next door, and the family was together. So, while it wasn't a house of our own, it was a very comfortable arrangement.

BRAINSTORM: VISITING THE DJs

During that time, my brother, Norm, bought a home-improvement business in Grand Rapids, and I really wanted to work for him. So I left my job with the Lenderinks to work for Norm while traveling occasionally to concert bookings. Trent and I were trying to sock away some savings so we could build our own home *and* promote my music career.

Soon after the first album was released, Trent had to go to Germany for two weeks, and before he left, I had a brainstorm. I said, "Trent, I'm going to get in the car and drive to every radio station I can see in the two weeks you'll be gone. Otherwise, I'll just be here missing you, and I don't have any bookings, so that's what I want to do."

He said, "That's a great idea, honey. I know if these people could just meet you, they will like you. Just be careful."

I got out a map and planned a big, circular route. My brother let me use his office phone, and I started calling Christian radio stations along the route to say, "I'm going to be passing through on this date, and I wonder if I could stop by to say hello." By that time I was familiar with a lot of the Christian hit radio station DJs, and I wanted to meet them and thank them for playing my music. Plus, I wanted to meet the guys and girls at adult contemporary radio just to say, "Hi, this is who I am. Here's my music. Would you consider giving it a try?"

I was totally on my own, financing the whole thing myself and traveling alone. The record company wasn't involved. I got in Trent's cute little Thunderbird supercoupe speedster, and I drove from Michigan down to Texas and over to Louisiana then on into Florida and all the way back up again, stopping in South Bend, Indiana, before I made it back to Grand Rapids. In two weeks' time, I visited more than fifty radio stations and a bunch of Christian bookstores.

If it was a CHR station, they might put me on the air, and the DJs and I would talk about my music and what I was doing. I'd tell them, "Thanks for playing my songs; I appreciate it." And I'd leave more of my music with them.

Then maybe an hour up the road, there would be an AC station, and I'd go in and explain that I didn't expect them to put me on the air, but I was just stopping by to say hi. "I'm an artist on REX," I would tell them, "and I had a radio hit on CHR. I know it's not really your format, but I just wanted to say hi so you can put a face with the name. And, here, I'd like to leave some product with you."

Some of the AC stations wouldn't let me get past the lobby, even though I had called ahead and set up a time to meet the DJ. I would tell the receptionist, "I'm just here to see so-and-so," and she would respond, "He's in a meeting. You can just leave your stuff with me."

I would smile, hand over the CDs, and say, "Sure, just tell him Tammy Trent stopped by to meet him."

The most memorable experience along those lines was at KSBJ, the biggest Christian station in Houston. They barely let me through the front door! Although I knew I shouldn't take those situations personally, it definitely hurt. But I managed to shrug it off, knowing it's just the way things are in this business. I got back in the Thunderbird and headed on down the road.

Other times the AC station DJs would agree to see me, "but just for a minute." Then, after we had talked awhile, they might say to me, "Do you have time to go on the air with us?" And of course I would say yes, thrilled at their change of heart.

I tried to see at least three stations a day. I would drive to the town where I was going to be, and I'd go to the first station at seven or eight in the morning, whenever the DJs were going to be on. I would stay as long as they would have me. Then I would get back in the car and drive maybe two hours to the next station. By then it was noon or early afternoon. Then I would try to get to the next station by four or so.

From there I might drive four or five hours to the next city. My constant thoughts were, *How can I make this happen? How can I meet these people? How can I push my career forward?*

Two weeks later I rolled back into Michigan, exhausted but feeling good about the groundwork I had laid.

"WHO *IS* THIS GIRL?"

Soon after that round of visits, REX released the next single. It was more of an AC kind of song, but it wasn't a success on AC radio. In 1996, I began work on my second album.

At about this point in my career, a company called Platinum Entertainment bought out REX Music and its sister company, Light Records. The new owners moved me over to Light. It was a label that had been around for a very long time but by then was mostly catalog music. Light didn't have any new artists, and Platinum was hoping to build up the artist roster again. My second album, *You Have My Heart*, was released under the Light label, and it was a success that opened up tremendous opportunities for me.

The first single released off that second album was "Welcome Home," which, since then, has become my signature song. One of the stations Light Records sent it to was KLTY in Dallas, the biggest Christian station in the country. Jon Rivers was the program director

This 1985 photo was taken during high school, about a year after we met. I knew then that Trent was the one for me.

The handsome Lenderink brothers as teenagers on a family trip to the Bahamas: Troy (left), Trent, and Tate. They loved diving together.

Trent and his dad, Tom Lenderink, flying off on one of their many adventures together to some exotic or mysterious place. Since he'd been a little boy, Trent had loved traveling with his dad.

I almost ruined Trent's surprise when he arranged to give me my engagement ring in a Happy Meal at McDonald's. Afterward, we went to Goggy and Poppy's house and took this picture.

As we came into the wedding reception, the first thing Trent did was lead our guests in a prayer. I remember him thanking the Lord for his new bride, Tammy Lenderink. I was in heaven!

The happiest day of my life with Trent. Right after we were married on August 18, 1990, at First Assembly of God in Grand Rapids, we took pictures in the church's beautiful courtyard.

For our first anniversary, Trent took me to Cancun, Mexico. We would later return to Cancun many times as we owned a time-share there right on the beach.

Trent and I worked together in his family's wood products business. Our work spaces were on opposite ends of the building, but I tried to lure him into my office from time to time for a quick kiss.

Trent and his nephews Kenny (right) and Kyle share ice cream cones
during our vacation together in Florida. This was a surprise trip for the
little boys, and another part of the surprise came when they found out
Uncle Trent and Aunt Tammy were meeting them in Orlando.

For our tenth anniversary, Trent surprised me with a trip to Hawaii, where he had taken me on our amazing honeymoon.

To let me know he was thinking of me even while he was on vacation, Trent, still a teenager, wrote this underwater note—"I Love Tam"—while diving with his brothers during a family vacation. I still have the note today.

Trent was never afraid when he was diving, even when sharks came by to get acquainted. He was so proud of this picture. He didn't tell me about this adventure until *after* the dive.

At the resort in Jamaica, a hotel photographer took this photo of us—our last photo together.

My brother-in-law, Ken Hass, and I ran in the Olympic Torch Relay Run in Nashville before the 2002 Olympics. I ran in Trent's place, and Ken, at the last minute, was asked to run with me.

At Trent's gravesite, we left (from top of photo) a plastic bag filled with
photos of the two of us and our home, along with some other little
favorite things: a note from my sister, Gina; a red rose; a roll of his
favorite Polo candy from England; Wang toys that Trent had invented;
a "Living H2O" T-shirt Trent and I had made and sold; and seventeen
boxes of Nerds.

there, and other stations watched what he was playing, then they would play it too. If Jon Rivers played a song, everybody played it. So it was a wonderful surprise when someone from Light called me and said, "Tammy, you've got to listen to this voice mail message we got from Jon Rivers." They transferred me to the message, and there was Jon, saying, "Who *is* this girl? This is one of the greatest songs I've heard in a long time. We are adding it" (radio talk meaning the station had decided to start playing it).

"Welcome Home" ended up charting up to number seven on AC—my first AC hit. The song was a major success for me, and one of the reasons it happened was because of all those DJs I had met on my driving tour. A lot of them told me, "It's a good song, Tammy, and it meets our format, but another reason we played it was because we had met you and felt like we knew you. We know how hard you worked, driving around the country to meet us, and no other artists we know have done that on their own. You must be the hardest-working girl in Christian music."

"Welcome Home" did well in both CHR and AC. Then "Run to the Cross" was released, the second single sent out off that album, and it became a top-five hit; it even charted up to fifteen in another market, inspiration radio.

It was about then that Light Records got a call from KSBJ, the Houston station that wouldn't let me past the front desk when I stopped by to visit. Its staff wanted me to come to Houston to do a Brown Bag Lunch concert, a free event the radio station sponsored occasionally at one of the city's big malls. The record company would have to pay to send me down there, but the midday concerts were a huge draw, so they gladly agreed to do it.

The date would occur while I was on the Soul Revival Tour, but we managed to work out the schedule. I did the morning show at the radio station, then we went to the mall and did the concert for more than a thousand people. It was fun for everyone involved, so I wasn't all that surprised when they called later that year and said, "Could you come back and do another one?"

I've done a few more of those KSBJ Brown Bag Lunch concerts since then, and sometimes when they call to invite me back, I tease those DJs and remind them, "You guys wouldn't even let me in your front door!" We all get a laugh out of it now and our relationship is wonderful, but it was a hard thing when it happened. Christian artists try hard to get people in the industry to believe in them so they can entertain listeners while at the same time sharing how important it is, and how wonderful it is, to believe in Jesus. But when you can't get in the door, when you can't get the help you need, you sometimes just have to believe in yourself and promote yourself on your own.

This was my beginning as a professional recording artist. My bookings continued to increase, and I was on the road a lot while Trent stayed back home in Michigan with his family. In 1997, I was to tour the country with Petra, an all-guy Christian group, but I couldn't travel in their bus. Petra didn't allow girls on their bus with all the guys. So I would have to drive separately. Thinking about all those long drives and lonely nights, I said, "Trent, can you go with me? Can you become my manager? We can travel the world together; we'll be together all the time, and we'll have fun."

We were still living with his parents, and he was still working for the family business. Many times, he had expressed frustration about not knowing what purpose God had for his life. He had so much to give— so much talent and intelligence and personality—but in his career, he just wasn't fulfilled. He struggled with that dilemma a lot. He would say, "Tammy, you must feel wonderful because you *know* you're doing something for God. You're making a difference and sharing the gospel. I want to do something like that, something where I know I'm doing good and making a difference." Trent often asked himself—and God, in his prayers—"Lord, what am I supposed to do with my life? I want to do something for you, but I don't know what it is."

Now I begged him, "Come with me, Trent. I know it will be hard to leave the family business. I know you'll feel like you're letting down your family, disappointing them somehow. But Trent, I need you, and this might be an opportunity to find what else is out there for you."

So he came with me, and we set off on an exciting new chapter of our lives. But there was a downside to my growing success . . .

8

I would bring Trent up on the platform at every concert and make him sing to the crowd. The audience always loved his off-key rendition of "Happy Birthday to You."

8 | on our own

_H_AVING TRENT WITH ME CHANGED EVERYTHING—because he _handled_ everything: all the details and all the travel arrangements. I loved it. We had a booking agent, but he did the day-to-day scheduling and handled the bookings that came to us directly. He was the liaison with the outside booking agent, as well, approving dates and arranging interviews. He worked with the pastors at churches where I would be performing and made all the hotel and airline reservations. He helped with packing all the equipment I would need and the merchandise we would sell. I knew when we settled into our seats on the plane or in the car that he had taken care of every last detail. It was awesome having him with me.

During the concert he was always at the soundboard with the sound technician. It was so reassuring to look back there, over the heads of the audience members, and see him back there, my steady, handsome, dependable Trent. When things went especially well and the crowd was cheering, he would flash his beautiful smile at me as if to say, _That's my girl._

Trent was always my biggest supporter in every way. He knew all my music, all the performance tracks I used as accompaniment, and he knew exactly when to do what. When Trent was there, I didn't worry; I knew everything would go smoothly. He would signal the sound technician when it was time to play a certain track or to do whatever needed to be done to make the show run smoothly.

TRENT'S VOICE IN MY EAR

When I'm performing onstage, I usually wear an ear monitor, as most entertainers do. The monitor lets me hear the accompaniment better, and it also lets the soundboard guy talk to me in case there's something important I need to know. It doesn't happen very often, because, as you might imagine, it's very distracting to have someone talking in your ear while you're singing or talking to hundreds of people. Trent knew that, but sometimes, back there at the soundboard, he just couldn't resist. Maybe, during applause, he might say in my ear, "Awesome, girl! That was great." Other times he said things he knew would make me laugh: "Oh, girl, you look hot tonight. I can't wait to be with you later."

No one else could hear because he would have the soundboard mike, and it was going only to my ear monitor. It was cute, and I loved it, but sometimes I would be so thrown off that I was totally distracted. He knew not to do it every show, because he figured out, *She's gonna get mad if I keep doing this.* But it was fun for him, so every once in a while, maybe when I was laughing or when a song had just ended, he would whisper something. One time he did it again, and I glared back at the soundboard and said, "Trent, stop it!" Then I looked back at the audience and explained, "He's whispering things in my ear, and I can't concentrate. Now, Trent, stop it!"

Well, the audience loved it! Everyone turned to look at my handsome husband standing back there smiling like the cat that just ate the canary, and they roared with laugher.

Realizing that people wanted to see and know more about him, I started bringing Trent up on stage. Usually I introduced that part of the program by talking about dating and the importance of sexual purity. I painted an elaborate picture of Trent, telling them how, even when I might have yielded during our seven and a half years of dating, he was the strong one. I shared how he would say to me, "Girl, you're going to be so glad we waited," and how true that was. Then I would ask, "Do you guys want to meet this incredible man?" and the crowd would applaud. I always thought that, after my little buildup about waiting and his strength in maintaining sexual purity, they would expect some dopey-looking guy. Then this gorgeous hunk of a man walks up from the soundboard, climbs onto the stage, and the girls especially were going, *Wow!* Everyone would cheer and hoot when they saw him.

I would sit him down on a stool, and we would have this cute little dialogue with each other. We would do it at every show, but the audience probably thought, *Poor Trent! She's really putting him on the spot.*

I would tell the listeners, "You'll be happy to know that I am the singer in the family, because Trent can't sing—cannot sing at all. In fact, he is completely tone deaf."

Trent would huff, "I am *not* tone deaf!"

"Yes, you are, Trent," I would argue.

"I'm not tone deaf," he would say. "I can hear the notes; I just can't *sing* the notes."

"Baby, that's tone deaf," I would explain.

People would be laughing and chuckling, and I would keep going: "OK, Trent, well, I was just thinking it would be really nice if you could sing for me—sing for us tonight." He would say, "No! No way!" but of course the audience would cheer for him to do it.

Then I would ask, "Is there somebody here who has a birthday tonight—or maybe a birthday in the last year? OK, what's your name?" Maybe it was Jennifer. I would tell Trent, "OK, Trent, we're going to sing 'Happy Birthday' to Jennifer."

"OK."

"Now, Trent, you just follow me. I'm gonna start you out, then you just pick up on it and finish it, and you'll sing 'Happy Birthday' to Jennifer."

We would make a start, and Trent would grimace and say, "Tammy, you had to pick one of the most difficult songs to sing!"

"Oh, Trent! It is not. OK, here we go: 'Hap—.'"

Trent would complain, "Well, you've gotta give me more than *that!*"

I'd sing, "Hap-py . . ."

He would follow: "Hap-py . . . " And off he would go, singing

"Happy Birthday" to Jennifer completely off key. It was always painful to hear. Then I would say, "Did you just *wink* at her? Trent, I think you winked at her! Did you wink at her?"

The crowd would be laughing, and we would hug. On stage, he always hugged me in the same sweet way. He would reach over and hug me around my back, and he'd put his hand on the back of my head and pull me into him. He would give me a little kiss, and whisper, so no one else knew he was doing it, "I love you."

Then he would head back to the soundboard, and I would tell the audience, "Isn't he great? What a gift from God he is—so yummy."

When the program ended, we would head for the merchandise table and work side by side selling my products. Over and over again while I was autographing, Trent would be asked to sign too. He always wrote, "Rock on! Love, Trent."

RESISTING CHANGE

Platinum wanted to expand and move into the secular market, and as part of that plan, it rereleased my song "Welcome Home" to secular radio throughout the country. Surprisingly, it actually made it onto one of the secular charts—somewhere in the thirties, right below a Madonna song. Because it did fairly well, Platinum, the parent company, was convinced I needed to do a whole secular album.

They really pushed me to do it, but I just felt uncomfortable with the idea. Trent and I went to a meeting with some of the label executives, and they were very persuasive, but after we left the meeting, I told Trent, "This is just not what I want to do. I can't explain it, really. It might be an awesome opportunity, I don't know, but I'm no good at that stuff. I don't fit there. I know other Christian artists have crossed over—Amy Grant and dc Talk and some of the others, but Trent, I just feel like I'll be eaten alive if I try that."

Trent said, "If you really mean it—if it's really what you want—then I'll get you out of this, Tammy."

We were at a standstill: Platinum said either I would do the secular record, or I wouldn't do anything. I was still under contract with the company for another record, and if that record wasn't aimed at the secular market, their attitude was, *Then you'll sit, and you'll wait.*

I begged Platinum executives to let me out of the contract, and they said, "Sure—for a buyout."

I argued, "I don't have that kind of money, and I can't make you any money, because I don't want to do a secular record. So won't you please, please, please let me out of this deal?"

The executives wouldn't budge, but I didn't give up. Every week or so I would call the company president and leave a message saying, "Hi, this is Tammy Trent. I would love it if you could just consider letting me out of this deal." He never returned my calls, but I kept leaving him the messages. I prayed and I called and I prayed and I called, and finally one day he called me back.

"What is it exactly that you want, Tammy?" he asked.

"I want out of the deal," I told him.

"OK. You're out of the deal."

I was so relieved, I cried! Finally, an answer to my prayers.

But then nothing happened. The president didn't follow up, and the contract remained in force.

We continued our prayers over the next days and weeks, always hoping that somehow I could be released from the contract. But while our hopes were high, we knew the odds were against us. Everyone in the music industry knew other singers and groups that had been in similar situations and ended up having to spend thousands of dollars to buy out their record contracts so they could be free to do what they wanted. I was just the next artist in line, waiting and hoping. All we could do was put it in God's hands and know that whatever happened next would be his will.

Trent and I were in California about a month later when my attorney called us. "You are not going to believe this," she said. "I am holding in my hand the letter we sent to your record company six months ago, asking them to sign it and release you. It just came back today. They signed it, releasing you from everything. You're free, Tammy. You owe them nothing."

We were beside ourselves, relieved and thankful and once again seeing that things happen in God's timing, not ours.

It was time for a break, time to set off in a new direction. In early 1999, I got a deal with Nashville-based Sparrow Records, and after a lot of prayer and talking—and with Trent doing tons of research, of course, into every possibility—we decided it was time to leave Michigan and move to Nashville. We would be closer to the record company, closer to the booking agent, and after five years of living with his parents, we would truly be on our own.

We flew down in late 1998 and started looking for a place to live. Trent's research showed us what would be the best area of Nashville for us, and we considered all the different possibilities: apartments, condos, building new, buying something used. We looked at dozens of places, and Trent was completely unselfish in how we decided what to do. There was no tension in the process of deciding. He simply wanted the best for me in everything, and if I said, "I don't like this," he didn't argue with me, even if it was a house he liked. He was always a great listener. When I pointed out flaws or things I didn't like, he would say, "You're probably right. Let's keep looking until we find something we both think is the one for us."

It took a lot of looking, but we finally found it—a model home we walked into and immediately said together, "This is it." In April, we bought the lot and signed the contract, and in November 1999, we loaded up our things and moved out of his family's home. I know it was hard for his family; Mom Lenderink cried as we drove away. We felt sad to leave but excited to be moving into our dream home in a suburb of Nashville.

Who could have known the dream would last less than two years?

9

After a concert in Florida, Trent had to leave early to catch a flight for a scuba diving trip to Cancun, Mexico, with his buddies. When I was ready to leave, I found this note under the windshield wiper of the rental car:

9 | marriage and music, nashville style

M Y CONTRACT WITH SPARROW RECORDS would result in a song that charted number one nationwide on adult contemporary Christian radio. But from the start, the relationship was touch and go. As one of its first requests of me, Sparrow asked me to consider finding a new manager.

It broke my heart, but Trent and I both understood. Record executives offer suggestions and sometimes criticism to an artist's manager. They lay out what they need and expect the manager to guide the artist to conform. But when, in those negotiations, the executives are not saying, "Your artist needs to change something," but "Your *wife* needs to change something," well, it's obviously awkward.

Trent didn't hesitate, didn't complain. He just said, "OK, Tammy, let's listen to their counsel and get outside management for you."

It was very hard for me after that to attend meetings with Sparrow and have Trent waiting outside. But he was always so good about it. He'd just say, "I'll just wait here; everything's fine. Don't worry."

But I kept thinking, *This is not the way it's supposed to be. You and I have been in this together, and now it feels like they're saying you can't be a part of it, and I hate that!*"

Sparrow released my album *Set You Free*, and the single "My Irreplaceable" went to number one. With our new home in Nashville as our home base, I now was busy touring and performing, and Trent still traveled with me. He just wasn't involved in the dealings with the record company. Then Sparrow released the single "Without You" from the same album, and it became a top-ten hit. Trent and I were busy, productive, and happy.

Sometimes when we were together in our home, Trent would yell from the downstairs office, "Tammy Trent!"

I would hurry out from an upstairs bedroom to look over the banister. "What, Trent? What is it?"

"I love you!" he would gush. That was Trent.

KING AND QUEEN OF CARDS (AND NOTES)

Trent would leave little cards and notes for me to find around the house, and I would do the same for him. We were big on giving each other cards and notes and surprises. And we wouldn't just walk in and hand over the card. Oh, no. That wouldn't be nearly as much fun. Instead we hid our little surprises in places where we knew they would be found. Trent might tuck something under my pillow. I loved to hide a card in his Dopp kit sometimes when he had to travel without me. It wasn't unusual to open the refrigerator in the morning and find a card propped up against the orange juice, or to slip into bed at night and find a card leaning against the alarm clock.

I kept them all; they're saved in albums that I pull out from time to time, and what comfort it brings me now to remember where each one was hidden and when it was given. Right now I'm looking at one that says, "Every time I let my heart lead me . . . I always find yours." And underneath the card's printed message, Trent wrote, "And that has not been all bad! You're as special to me as anything in this earth. I pray for deep, true, honest love between us and peace in all of our relationship. Yours, Trent."

Another special memory came on my birthday in 2000. Trent left the house and was gone for several hours. When he came back he had my birthday presents, including a cute little Prada backpack purse from

Costco that I had been wanting but thought was too expensive. On the birthday card, he wrote, "My love for you will never become dull. Sometimes the trials of life blind my vision, but being with you and even running around town and secretly buying a gift for you makes me feel alive. And I love it. Love, Trent."

Reading that note now, I see again how unselfish Trent was. He was still struggling with knowing exactly how God wanted to use him, and yet he assured me that while he waited for God's vision, simply being with me was enough to make him feel happy and alive.

SEEKING GOD'S PURPOSE

Again and again, Trent would tell me he had prayed, "God, where am I going? What am I doing? How can I serve you with my life the way Tammy serves you with hers?"

Trent was so smart and so gifted he could have done anything—but he didn't know what to do. He even considered going to medical school, but he was afraid the long years of schooling might keep him apart from me, and he didn't want that.

When he was very young, he worked in fashion modeling. From those experiences he developed a fondness for acting and did a lot of drama activities in college. With his good looks and natural talent, he probably could have gotten involved in the film industry and become a star. In fact, he considered going to Hollywood at one point, but knowing that he might have to compromise his values and beliefs, he didn't consider the idea long.

I think that, if the truth were told, Trent's ultimate dream was to be Boyd Matson, the host of *National Geographic Explorer* nature series. He loved animals and loved telling me (and anyone else) everything he knew about them. He would set up the camera on a tripod and videotape himself outside introducing his imaginary viewers to one of the marvels of nature. I would be inside cooking dinner and hear him out on the patio, saying, "Hi, I'm Trent Lenderink, and here's a little spider here, and here's a spider here, and see? They're mating. See that? See his little feet.

See that little smile on his face?" (If you have watched as many nature shows as I had to watch with Trent, you know, too, that you can't have one of these programs without having a mating scene.) I would laugh and yell at him, "Trent! Come inside for dinner!"

One time I agreed to help him do one of his videotaped nature profiles. The idea was that he would *run* up to the camera to greet the "audience" and show the viewers what an exciting show this was going to be. So here he came, running toward the camera, just a bit out of breath, wheezing, "Hi! I'm Trent Lenderink," and suddenly, *whump!* He tripped over something and fell flat. It's impossible to watch that videotape today without laughing hysterically.

He really practiced his nature shows, maybe thinking that one day he might audition for something somewhere. When Trent had an idea, he didn't just sit back and dream. He acted it out; he took steps toward making it happen. Those videotapes were his way of teaching himself how to present the best image and tell the best story on camera. He wanted to have a series called Trent TV, and knowing he would probably make it happen eventually, he had that name reserved for a future Website.

Trent was fascinated by the world of nature; he loved bugs and animals of every kind. Growing up in Michigan, he'd had a hobby room, and it was the first place he took me when I visited his home. He had a little baby alligator (he fed it goldfish!), and he had tarantulas. At one point he had a fourteen-foot python named Clarence that he would take to area elementary schools for informational programs. He wanted to show the kids how wonderful God's creation was. That's how much he loved both animals and children. He also would do science experiments down there in the Lenderinks' basement—the mad scientist at work. It's still funny to hear his family describing all the things he managed to accidentally blow up down there in his hobby room.

I am convinced that Trent was simply a genius, and he was an entrepreneur too, following in his father's footsteps. When we were out touring and giving concerts, I would sell lots of jewelry-type trinkets at my merchandise table. Early on, Trent looked at what I was selling, saw what I was paying my supplier for it, and said, "Girl, I can make this stuff for you, and it won't cost you nearly as much."

Once again he did his research, made contacts in Asia and within the United States, and developed his own products. We started selling them around the country wherever I performed, and when I was touring with other artists, they noticed the cool things at my table and wanted Trent to make things for them as well. He ended up developing his own catalog and set up a Website. He called the business ID Wear: Identify Your Faith, and he set as its motto the verse from Deuteronomy 6 that says of God's commandments: "Tie them as symbols on your hands and bind them on your foreheads."

His mom and other workers in the Lenderink offices helped him assemble the items, and they warehoused the products there. In just a short while, they were processing all sorts of orders and shipping out thousands of Trent's merchandise items. Trent had great ideas, and they quickly caught on. His little company is still thriving today.

INTRODUCING . . . THE LOG FAMILY

Trent was also an author. Yes, indeed! He wrote a book about . . . are you ready for this? Potty-training.

It's called *The Log Family*, and it's about a family of, uh, *logs* that liked to visit the stars of the book, Kenny and Kyle (named for my sister and brother-in-law's two boys, Trent's godsons). The little guys adored their Uncle Trent, and after he watched how hard it was for Kyle to get the hang of being potty-trained, he wrote this book to help him through this early challenge. And it worked! Gina and Ken insist Trent's book helped them turn the corner in getting little Kyle potty-trained.

Trent even researched artists and cartoonists and had illustrations done for the book. It is the funniest thing. The book begins by introducing a Chicago family that includes two brothers, Kenny and Kyle, who learned all about the Log family from their Uncle Trent, who is "a really cool but kind of weird scientist." The story begins with Uncle Trent explaining to Kenny and Kyle, "When we go number two in the bathroom, we have a chance to have a short but pleasant time with the Log family."

The silly story goes on to say that "often before the Log family comes to visit, they like to let you know. So they yell little messages out of your bottom. Kyle's messages sound like short pops. Kenny's messages are longer whistling sounds."

When the Log family comes to visit, their favorite way to play is "to take a dip in their favorite swimming pool. Uncle Trent says it took many years to develop swimming pools that the Log family likes best. . . . So whenever they come to visit, we should always get to one of the special swimming pools. After a short dip in the swimming pool, all Log families can't wait to take a ride on the water slide."

The book goes on to describe the "button that activates the water slide" and takes the Log family to "the beach." Next comes a little discussion about the correct amount of "beach towels" the family needs and how important it is not to load them down because their arms are too short to take along a heavy load of towels.

The best way to give the Log family a proper sendoff, Trent wrote, is to activate the "water slide" and yell, "See ya at the beach!"

Trent wrote this book and read it to Kyle again and again. As you can imagine, it was one of the little guy's favorite bedtime stories! It not only potty-trained him, it taught him to flush the commode. So now when it's quiet sometimes at Gina and Ken's house, one of the boys will be in the bathroom, and they'll hear the commode flush and Kyle or Kenny yelling, "See ya at the beach!"

DEALING WITH FRUSTRATION

There was nothing Trent couldn't do—except, perhaps, criticize me. I was (and will always be!) a *long* way from perfect. And one of the things I've always had trouble with is getting easily frustrated. Not that you would ever see it if all you know of me is the image I present on stage. Trent knew the deepest parts of me; he knew that while I buried my emotions in public, I felt safe, with him, to vent and let loose some of the pent-up feelings that had built up. This wasn't something that happened more than a dozen times in our marriage, but when it *did* happen—when I lost my temper—there would be a few minutes of what probably seemed to any other person in the room (usually Trent or another member of my family) like a good time to seek cover!

For example, if you and I were out for a drive, and somehow I dented my car, I might say, "Oh, man! I dented my car. That's awful. But thank heaven, I have insurance to take care of it." Then I would feel sad and drive off to the insurance office to get it taken care of.

But if it happened while I was driving with Trent, I would probably rant and rave for hours: "Oh, my gosh! Look at that! I've dented my car! God, why is this happening to me? Why would you let this happen to me? I can't believe this! My car! Look at my car! It's ruined!"

It's hard to explain why those of us who struggle with this problem shield it from strangers but unload it on the ones we love most. Someone told me a story once that helped me understand. A little boy's parents were getting divorced; the dad had walked out on the family and moved in with the girlfriend. Whenever the dad would come to visit the boy or take him out for the day, the little guy was always on his best behavior. He never complained, never raised a fuss about anything. But while he was home with his mom he could be a holy terror—yelling and arguing and getting into all sorts of trouble.

One night at bedtime, his mom tucked him in and said, "Jimmy, your dad tells me when you're with him, you're the best kid on earth. But when you're here with me, it seems you get so mad and you yell and argue with me at the drop of a hat. Why are you so good when you're with your dad and so angry all the time when you're with me?"

The little boy was quiet for a while then he said, "I guess it's because I can say what I feel and know that you'll stay. *You* won't ever leave me, will you, Mom?"

Maybe that's why we unleash our emotions on our closest family members while we're on our best behavior with outsiders. It doesn't make the angry outbursts easier for the loved ones to take, but it has helped me understand why I do what I do. That's how I was with Trent. When I lost my temper, I knew he wouldn't leave me. And he knew that wasn't how I really felt about him or the rest of the world. He knew I was "having a moment," as we used to say. And he loved me anyway.

But at the same time, he wanted the best for me, and he knew that holding in my feelings for a long time and then having them explode over some little problem *wasn't* the best. And Trent *always* wanted whatever would be beneficial for me. So, in his gentle way, he would make little suggestions. Once when we were shopping in a bookstore I found him in the "anger" section. He was looking at a book, and he held it up for me to see. "Could I buy you this book, Tammy? Would you read it?" When he saw the look on my face, he said, "Honey, it's not about me. I can handle anything, but I just want you to be happy. I want you to know freedom. I don't want you to be bound by this anger."

He told me, "Anger affects a lot of things, Tammy. It can affect your health. I love you, and I'm not trying to preach at you, but I think it would be so good if you would just read it. Could I buy it for you?"

I said, "Sure, Trent. Buy it for me." So he bought the book, and I read it. But I didn't work on the problem as much as I should have.

Trent never let it show that I had hurt him, but I know I did. In my anger, I would say things to Trent that I certainly didn't mean, things that had nothing to do with him. He knew that, and he was the first to forgive me. But even without his saying, "You're hurting me," I could see it in his eyes. Then immediately I would say, "Trent, I'm sorry. Please forgive me."

And he would always say, "I do, Tammy. You know I do."

I remember one time when I was stressed out about something the record company had done—some unfulfilled promise or some other way I'd been let down—I was ranting and raving around the house. Trent did what he could to pacify me, but when nothing worked, he went into the office, which is off the living room, and during my next pass in that direction he popped out the door and handed me the phone.

"What?" I snapped.

"It's your mother. Talk to her."

Trent knew that if anybody could calm me down, it was my mom. He also knew I would break down with Mom. He saw that I was trying to be Miss Tough Girl about the problem, angry and mad, when what I really felt was hurt. So he called my mom and told her what was happening. As soon as I held the phone to my ear and heard her say, "Honey, what's wrong?" the wall came down and the tears began to fall. It was what I had needed to do—have a good cry. But for some reason, I just hadn't been able to let go, and I had masked my sadness with anger that I unleashed upon poor Trent.

There's something else that I regret now. Trent always wanted me to need him. And I *did* need him. But there were a few times during our marriage when I just had a stubborn, independent streak, and I would tell him, "I don't need you to do this, Trent. I can do this by myself. I can do this on my own. You don't have to save me from everything, Trent."

And he would say simply, "OK, Tammy. Fine. Do it yourself."

One of those times happened in Orlando when I was to perform there. We got into some little tiff in the hotel room—I'm sure I was the one who started it, whatever it was—and I told Trent, "I don't need you. I can do this myself."

He said, "Fine! Then go do it yourself."

I said, "Fine! I will."

I got in the car and drove over to the place where the event was being held. I set up my own merchandise, set up my own backdrop (something I had never done before), and all the time I was trying to figure out how Trent did everything while fighting to hold back the tears and thinking, *What have I done? I do need him. I can't do this alone.* Then I put on my happy face and went out there to sing to a packed house. That night there was no Trent to call up on the stage. No sweet, handsome man standing back at the soundboard. And there was no way I could get up there and perform and not worry about the program going smoothly; I worried about everything that night. I was on my own—and I didn't like it.

After the concert, I worked the merchandise table with several volunteers. Then, when the doors closed, I packed up the backdrop and everything else, and I drove back to the hotel. Trent was sitting at the desk, working on the computer. He looked up briefly when I walked in. "How'd it go?" he asked pleasantly.

"It was good," I said. "It was good."

"That's good," he answered. (We liked that word *good*.)

"Did you figure out the backdrop?"

"Uh-huh, I did."

Then he went back to his computer, leaving me standing there in the middle of the room, knowing there was more to be said. "Trent, I'm so sorry." The words came rushing out, and the tears I'd been holding back started to flow. "I'm so sorry. You know I need you. You know I can't do this without you."

That night was a lesson for me. Trent would never say it out loud, but the message was, *You said it one too many times, Tammy. Go do it yourself. And in the future, be careful what you say.*

Trent let me know that he would always be there for me. And he also let me see that, yes, I *could* do it myself. But oh, how much better it was when he was with me!

SPEAK LIFE

In so many ways, Trent was a man of God. Of all his wonderful characteristics and talents, that one was most important to me. Faithful and consistent, he guided me gently toward the things of God. One of the ways he did this was by teaching me how powerful our words can be. There's life in our words, or there's death. Trent's words always spoke life into me. They always encouraged me, supported me, empowered me. In eleven years of marriage, I can never remember Trent saying a hateful word to me. One of my biggest regrets is that I didn't always do the same for him.

People have asked me, when I go on and on like this about Trent, "Surely he had some faults—some little irritating things he did."

Well, yes, he wasn't perfect. He messed up the checkbook a time or two. He was great at numbers but hated keeping track of the checks. So I was the keeper of the checkbook, and I wanted every single penny accounted for and every check recorded. Those things weren't all that important to Trent. But no, he wasn't the one who left the cap off the toothpaste; that was me. He would brush his teeth, and when he was done he would rinse the toothbrush and wipe the handle, then take the towel and wipe the sink. In contrast, I would brush, spit, and walk away. He wasn't a nagger, but sometimes he would say, "Tammy couldn't you just wipe off the sink just a little bit?"

I'd say, "I'm sorry Trent. But, baby, this is my sink; that's your sink. Yours is clean; mine is the way it is."

He'd smile and say OK.

And, girls, here's something else remarkable about Trent: I can't recall a single time when he left the toilet seat up!

Can you see why I am still head-over-heals in love with this guy? He spoke life into me. He took my anger and never turned it back on me. And he wanted nothing more than for me to shine and to grow in spirit and in my walk with the Lord. He wanted to teach me everything he knew—but I balked at learning. Sometimes Trent tried to show me how to do something so I could do it myself if I needed to—fix a leaky faucet or set up new software on the computer or fold up the new backdrop for concerts, and I'd refuse to let him teach me.

"Trent, I don't want to know. Don't tell me. You can always do it for me," I would say. "I don't need to know, Trent, because you're always going to be here."

10

Dear Tammy,

I just returned home from the Women of Faith conference. . . . Although the entire conference was a blessing, your story touched my heart and changed my life . . . because I saw how we are not promised tomorrow. We are so blessed each day to share those moments with the ones we love. I could not wait to get home and hold my husband and two little girls in my arms.

Thank you, Tammy, for helping me find the love that so often gets lost through years of life, struggles, and pain. Thank you for rejuvenating the passion that led my heart to fall so deeply in love with my husband. Thank you for showing me the strength of God.

Robin Hambright,
Floydada, Texas

P.S. My husband thanks you too! Since I've been home, I can't keep my hands off him!!!

10 | At the crossroads

*M*Y CONTRACT WITH SPARROW had produced some major successes, but as the time neared for the contract to expire, I think we were all having some second thoughts about renewing it. There had certainly been disappointments on my side of the table, and perhaps Sparrow felt the same way, for some reason I didn't know. In the end, the label asked me to sign a ninety-day extension while company executives decided whether they wanted to do another record with me.

Trent and I talked it over, and I finally told Sparrow, "It's obvious you don't completely believe in me. So I don't see any point in signing this ninety-day extension. You can just drop me now."

And that's what happened.

When we got the official notification that the contract had expired, Trent and I looked at each other and thought, *Now what?*

Trent was busy with a lot of things. He was working at the time with Teen Mania and Acquire the Fire, doing a lot of their merchandising. He was helping his dad design a golf course in Michigan, and, of course, he was writing his potty-training book (I'm smiling as I write that). I had enough bookings to keep my name out there before the public, even without a record contract. But now we were pondering together the questions Trent had struggled with for so long: *Lord, how can we serve you now? How can we find your purpose for our lives?*

We seemed to be at a crossroads, an intersection in my career, and the traffic light had turned red. It felt like a time and a place where we could take a break, step back a little, and just take some time to consider which way to go.

In addition to being without a record contract again, we had been through a major family upheaval in the last few years, and I was still reeling from it emotionally. My mom had learned that throughout most of her marriage to Roger he had been unfaithful to her. It continued until the situation became absolutely impossible. Then they were divorced.

More than ever during that time, I was thankful to have Trent in my life; my relationship with him was the only normal relationship I'd ever had with a man. He was the only man who both loved me with all his being *and* was totally there for me.

At that time, I made a choice to let go of Roger altogether. I loved him and cared about him, and I knew he had loved me the best he could. But he had not been an accepting, caring father figure to me, and my life will always hurt because of that; there will always be a painful void in my heart where a full-time dad's love should go. From that point on, I stopped calling him *Dad*. I have completely forgiven him and truly do care about him. That I've been able to do so is the real story of God's love. But I no longer consider him my father today.

AN EXPANDED FAMILY, RESTORED

After she and Roger divorced, my mom stepped away from the speaking circuit. She went through a time of feeling really down, really depressed. But thank God she has made a marvelous comeback. She's speaking again—and what a testimony she has! She's sharing God's grace in her life and what he has brought her through. She's really a beautiful lady. And she has a wonderful new husband, Keith, who loves her generously and supportively and treats her like the special lady she truly is.

I love Keith, and I'm glad he's part of our family now. Best of all, we *are* a family again, thanks to Trent. On August 18, 2001, he worked a minor miracle that we're all very thankful for now.

That day I was performing at a big festival in Holland, Michigan, and both sets of my parents came: Dad and Valerie, Mom and Keith. The relationship between Dad and Mom had been strained ever since their divorce. While they never spoke negatively about each other in front of us kids, they both had difficult memories that kept them from being friends. They never socialized, and whenever they both ended up in the same room, there was always a lot of tension, although nothing was ever said. It was just a feeling that made everyone antsy.

That day at the festival, after I had finished singing, Mom came up to me and said, "Do you want to have dinner afterward?"

It was our eleventh wedding anniversary. I told Mom, yes, I'd love to; we would celebrate together. She said she and Keith would wait for me to finish signing autographs, then we would go to the restaurant. A few minutes later, my dad and Valerie came to see me backstage. "Would you like to go out with us to eat, Tammy?" Dad said. "We could celebrate your anniversary."

Uh-oh, what could I do? I said, "Oh, Dad, that sounds like fun. Let me just check with Trent and see. He might already have something planned." I knew I had to make a choice, one or the other, and I didn't know what to do.

I pulled Trent aside and said, "What do we do? They both want to go to dinner, and I don't want to hurt anyone's feelings. Oh, Trent, I just wish we could all go together—but I know that's impossible."

The line of autograph-seekers was growing. I had to get back to signing. Trent said, "I'll work it out. Don't worry. I'll think of something; just sign your autographs."

Holland isn't far away from Grand Rapids, so I had lots of friends there, and all of them had come, wanting to say hello. I ended up signing autographs and visiting with the folks in line for nearly two hours. And all the time I was wondering how Trent was going to "work it out."

Finally, he sent someone to pick me up in a golf cart and bring me to the green room, the backstage area where performers can relax. I hopped off the cart and opened the door to the green room, and there were *both* sets of my parents, with their spouses, and they were all talking to each other! They were smiling and laughing and obviously having a good time.

My mouth fell open, and tears filled my eyes. I couldn't believe it! I slipped up beside Trent and whispered in his ear, "Babe, what happened? What did you do?"

He said, "I just kinda talked to them and said, 'Why don't we all go out to eat?' I told them how wonderful that would be for us, how special it would be for you, and they all agreed."

So all six of us went out to dinner that night. At first it was a little uncomfortable. You could feel everyone holding back a little, waiting to see how things would unfold. But then the tension eased, and we all had a wonderful time.

I was on cloud nine, so happy to be in the midst of *all* my parents.

How amazing to look back now and see how God used Trent to help put my family back together. None of us knew then that in less than three weeks I would need them all, united and strong, during that darkest hour . . . when I lost him.

11

Rescue Me

I've been strong to give the world a song and
to sing praises to my King.
I've been there every time and the first one in line
when you've called.
But right now I can't imagine how I can live.
I got nothin' more to give.
I've been picked now to cope with the same path
of Job. Hear my fall.

I need you to rescue me from this feeling I won't
breathe again.
I need you to rescue me and make my spirit
strong within.

Jesus, show me you're here forever.
Jesus, hold me 'cause I need a savior.

—Tammy Trent & Pete Orta

11 the blue lagoon

*D*URING THE SUMMER OF 2001, that crossroads time of our life together, we took a break. There were plenty of bookings—I still had a full schedule—but there was no record contract, no album I had to be working on. So the pace was a little more relaxed, and we were having a lot of fun. We had worked some choreography into the program, and I was traveling with a couple of dancers. I loved getting to move around the stage with them, and the audiences ate it up.

As we traveled together that summer, Trent and I grew even closer, talking about our hopes and our dreams. We had always been snugglers; we constantly cuddled with each other, always holding hands and giving each other little pecks on the cheek. I loved to just stretch up and sniff Trent's ear. He always smelled so good! It was a common thing for people on airplanes to ask us if we were on our honeymoon. I always wanted to say, "No, but he's sure a yummy honey!"

We were loving and playful in our marriage. I adored Trent, and he adored me. After eleven years of marriage, despite some ups and downs, that hadn't changed. The way Trent loved me made me cherish him, respect him, and want to give to him, take care of him. Sometimes I felt I didn't deserve him.

On our way home from one concert that summer, Trent and I started talking about having children. Of course we had discussed it many times before, but we had always postponed starting a family because we were busy serving God in this music ministry that kept us on the road, away from home. That would be a tough way to raise children. But now, flying back to our beautiful new home in Nashville, we were rethinking that idea.

I suggested that we tap our savings and pay off our house—or come as close to that goal as possible. "If we didn't have the house payment—or if it was really low—and with all that you've got going now, maybe all I would have to do would be one or two bookings a month, and we could make ends meet," I told Trent. "If that's all the traveling we were doing, I'm sure we could figure out a way to take the baby on the road with us. And also, maybe you could pursue some more of the things you want to do."

He nodded, smiling. I could tell his mind was racing ahead—maybe he was thinking of reading *The Log Family* to his own three-year-old someday!

I rattled on, clinching the deal. "And if we had a baby, at least I would have a part of you if anything were ever to happen to you, Trent. And if anything ever happened to me, then you would have an extension of me."

Trent grinned, and his eyes flashed. He grabbed my hand and said, "That's it! We're starting a family right *now!*"

I laughed as he playfully reached over to get *both* his hands on me. "Trent, no! We're on an airplane!"

MAKING PLANS

It was a wonderful, busy summer, even though a thread of worry wove itself through our days. Sure, there were plenty of bookings now, but without a new album on the horizon, we couldn't help but wonder if the steady stream of dates might dry up. All we could do was keep working, keep taking our music to everyone who would have us. And like a pot of gold waiting at the end of the rainbow, there was a trip to Jamaica waiting for us at the end of the summer.

The trip would be an all-expenses-paid mission trip sponsored by Salem Communications to benefit an organization called Food for the Poor. They needed an artist who would go to Jamaica, observe how the ministry worked in third world conditions, and then come back and be a spokesperson for the group on Christian radio stations, including KLTY, the biggest Christian station in the country. I said I would love to do the trip.

Trent suggested we turn it into a vacation, switching our time-share to Jamaica for a week of fun and relaxing before moving on to Kingston to hook up with Food for the Poor. Once again he did tons of research and found a wonderful place that was all-inclusive; the package deal would include meals and all sorts of activities. We would pay for that first week of the trip, and when we moved on to Kingston, we would be the guests of Salem Communications and Food for the Poor.

So we worked hard all summer, and a few days before we left for Jamaica, we took two important steps: We sent a big check to the mortgage company to almost completely pay off our house. And we added maternity coverage to our insurance.

Eagerly, we packed for the trip. We always shared luggage; my stuff and Trent's things were all in the same suitcase. In his briefcase he carried his laptop and my booking schedule, something we took everywhere we went. The day after we returned from Jamaica, I would go right to a choreographed concert in Tupelo, Mississippi. Dancers had been booked to meet me there.

When I saw Trent dragging out his underwater scooter, I asked, "Trent, do you have to take that thing? Could we just go someplace without taking that?"

He said, "No, I'm taking it. It's fun, and I'll be diving while we're there. So it has to go."

"OK," I sighed, "but you'll have to load it and carry it, and you know how heavy it is."

"I know, I know," he answered.

Pam Thum and her husband, Steve, picked us up early that morning of September 3 to take us to the airport. When we heard the horn beep in the driveway, we picked up our bags and headed for the door. But right before we left, we paused, and Trent said, as he always did, "Thank you, Jesus, for our home. Protect it while we're gone. Thank you, God." The little ritual was as routine for us as locking the doors and setting the security system.

Trent had another little traveling ritual as our plane was taking off. As the engines revved for takeoff, he squeezed my hand and prayed, "Thank you, Jesus, for this day. Protect us, Lord, as we fly. In Jesus' name, amen." Others might cross their fingers and hope for the best. Trent put our lives in God's hands, and we felt no fear.

JAMAICA

I was so excited to be going to Jamaica knowing I had nothing to do for a whole week but just play with Trent. After the busy summer, I really needed to get away and relax. The fun started as soon as we landed and got into the rental car. In Jamaica, you drive on the left side of the road, and the steering wheel is on the right side of the car. Trent settled in on the "wrong" side of the front seat, and we laughed to discover the car was a stick shift.

Trent was fine at shifting through the forward gears with his left hand. But backing up was another matter. He just couldn't find reverse. Whenever it was time to back out of a parking spot, we would sit there in the car, going nowhere, while he tried and tried and tried—and finally gave up. "*You* put it in reverse," he said. So I became the reverse girl; when it was time to back up, Trent pushed in the clutch and yelled, "Reverse!" and I grabbed the shifter with my right hand and put the car into gear. It gave us a laugh every time we went anywhere.

The time-share resort offered lots of sport-focused activities we enjoyed together: basketball courts and a climbing wall, shuffleboard, tennis, swimming-pool volleyball. It even had a big trampoline anchored out in the surf. You could swim out there and play on it or lie out with the waves gently *swooshing* under you. One afternoon we were out there, lying out in the sun, and we fell asleep! By the time we woke up, the sun was going down. It was a little scary to me, but it was beautiful too. Trent said, "Tammy, we've gotta come out here one night and just sleep out here all night long."

"Huh-uh, Trent," I answered. "Not me!"

Trent hopped off the trampoline and treaded water, waiting for me to come down the ladder. I've always been the kind of girl who didn't want to ruin my makeup and get my hair wet. (I know, I know! It's silly, but that's just me.) The edge of the trampoline was padded and rounded, and my legs weren't long enough to get my feet over the edge and onto the ladder. Trent helped me in the sweetest way. He didn't say, "Don't be ridiculous! Just jump in! Who cares if your hair gets wet?" And he didn't say, "OK, figure it out yourself. I'm going in." Instead, he said, "OK, Tam, I'll go underwater and put my hands up. You put your feet in my hands, and I'll let you down." Just like my own private elevator.

Trent was my best friend. We could sit and talk for hours, and that's what we did during that week in Jamaica. One afternoon we were lying out on the beach, talking and enjoying the sunshine, when Trent spotted some boats and jet skis tearing through an area where several snorkelers were in the water. "What are they doing?" he fumed. "What a bunch of idiots! Don't they see the snorkelers out there?"

"The jet skis are so loud, Trent," I said. "Surely the swimmers will hear them."

"It's different underwater, Tam," he said. "You can hear the jet ski or the boat when you're underwater, but the sound is the same whether it's way over there—or right on top of you. It's the same volume. Unless you're watching, you just don't know. Those boats and jet skis shouldn't be in that swimming area."

Fortunately, no one was hurt, but it gave me something to think about the next day when Trent went on a dive. I wasn't feeling well that day—something I ate didn't agree with me—and Trent offered to change his plans and stay in the hotel room to keep me company.

"Trent, go," I said. "I would feel better knowing you're having fun. I'm just gonna stay in bed and watch TV. You go"

So he left, and I stood at the window, watching for him to emerge from the hotel lobby and turn back to wave—our thing. We never parted with just a good-bye kiss and a single wave. No, we were serial wavers. Even when getting on planes as one of us was leaving and the other was staying, the one who was leaving would turn and wave—*bye!*—and turn and wave again—*bye, bye!*—and on it went. It's a wonder we didn't miss every plane! So I stood in the window and watched for Trent, and there he was. I smiled, knowing he would turn. And he did . . .

I had brought a card to give to Trent while we were there. One morning at the resort I hid it in his Dopp kit before I ran to the lobby on an errand. The card said, "I was born to love you . . . my heart tells me so." Below that I wrote, "I'm so glad to be here with you and have all your attention. What a wonderful feeling. You're so amazing, especially when you hold me. Love you forever. Love, Tammy."

When I came back, I found Trent sitting on the edge of the bed, reading it. He was just sitting there, smiling, and opening and closing the card. He did that two or three times, then he just held it, reading the inside message again.

I said, "Trent, what are you doing?"

"Just reading this card. I love it, Tammy," he said. "Do you mean it?"

"Oh, yes, Trent, I do. My heart definitely tells me that."

"I love you too, Tammy."

"I know you do, honey."

It's such an important memory for me now, because it reassures me sometimes when I struggle with the thought that, sure, I know Trent loved me, but did he know how much I loved him? I don't have to rack my brain trying to remember the last time I told him. When those kinds of worries creep in, God gives me the memory of Trent sitting there reading and rereading that card, and I think, *Yeah, he knew.*

On our last morning at the resort, Trent asked me to pick up some pictures that had been taken the night before. While I picked up the photos, he would pack the car. When I met him in the parking lot, he had bought me a silly little souvenir. It was a little box made out of a coconut that says Jamaica. He said, "I just thought I'd get it for you. It's kind of quirky, but it's cute. I thought you might like it." And he'd bought me a KitKat candy bar too.

You won't be surprised to know I still have the little souvenir, but can you believe it? I still have that KitKat too!

We got in the car, I put it in reverse, and off we went. We would spend the night in Kingston, where we would meet up with the Food for the Poor representatives. But first, Trent wanted to go free diving in the Blue Lagoon.

It was about a three-hour drive, and we got a little lost on the way. There was a bit of a spat over the map. Trent tried to look at it while he was driving, then he gave up and said, "Here, will you look at this and find out where we are?" He shoved the unwieldy, unfolded map toward me.

I shoved it back. "No, Trent, I don't know where we're going. I won't be able to figure it out. Just stop and look at it yourself."

We finally got to the village we were looking for and followed the signs that took us down a little road leading to the Blue Lagoon. A spectacular house stood on the left side of the road—big and rambling with pillared porches extending over the water. "Wow, Trent, isn't that an incredible house?" I gushed.

"Oh, my gosh!" he said. "It really is."

"Wouldn't it be cool to live in a place like that?" I went on.

"Someday maybe we will, baby," Trent said, flashing that wide smile of his.

We parked the car and walked over to the water, watching all the people and boats at this remote little pocket of paradise. We peeked around a tree and saw the front of the house we'd driven by earlier. It seemed to float over the edge of the lagoon. We imagined what a breathtaking view its occupants must have.

There was a restaurant with open-air dining right over the water. It was the perfect place to have lunch. We sat at one of the tables, enjoying the spectacular view, nibbling away. Afterward we walked back to the car so Trent could put on his dive suit. When he had it halfway on, he stood up, reached for my hand, and we walked together down to the dock alongside the lagoon. Before he pulled up the zipper, I stopped him to take his picture. Oh, did he look yummy!

THE LAST WAVE GOOD-BYE

We settled onto the edge of the dock, dropping our feet into the clear, warm water. In the last year or so, Trent had taught himself to free dive. He had done his usual research, then he had practiced in the bathtub.

I had always loved baths, and I loved them even more after we got married, because Trent and I took them together. It wasn't a sexual thing but something fun and relaxing. I'd fill the bathtub and light some candles. He would slide in with me, and we'd sit there and talk. He would wash my back, then we would turn around so I could wash his. After a while I would get out, and Trent would say, "I'm gonna stay in and practice awhile." Then he would slide under the water and practice holding his breath. He didn't gulp in a huge gasp and duck his face in the water. Instead he drew in a slow, deep breath and slid easily beneath the surface.

Whenever Trent was free diving (in places outside the bathtub), he usually went at least a hundred feet deep; he checked his depth by the indicator on his dive watch. Trent didn't take risks when he was diving. He was very smart that way. He wasn't one to be constantly pushing the envelope, because he never wanted to do anything that would scare me or cause me to worry. He told me once, "I don't want to do anything stupid that would cause you to have to live without me, Tammy. There are a lot of things I can do that are adventurous that I can do without causing you to be afraid."

So I wasn't worried at all as Trent prepared to dive that day. I sat beside him as he pulled on his fins, adjusted his mask and snorkel, eased the underwater scooter over the side of the dock, then slid quietly into the water without a splash, as easily and smoothly as an otter.

We talked a minute more as he treaded water, then he smiled at me and turned toward the lagoon. "OK. I'll be back in a little bit," he said. "Then we can do something *you* want to do. I'll see you in fifteen minutes."

"OK, Trent."

He pushed off, his body moving across the surface of the water as the little scooter pulled him toward the center of the lagoon. He kicked gently with the fins, his face in the water, as he glided away from me. I waited for him to stop, turn back, and wave. And there it was. He stopped in the water, just at the point where the clear, aquamarine shallows shaded into the deeper blue. His face, encased in the mask, came up out of water, the snorkel protruding past his ear. He turned back to me, lifted his hand beside his head, and quickly bent his fingers forward and up, forward and up. The silly little wave I'd seen a million times in all sorts of places. His wide smile appeared beneath the mask. I smiled back at him, lifted my hand beside my ear, and mimicked his finger-flapping in the same tight little motion.

Then Trent turned back toward the deep water, sank beneath the surface, and was gone.

It was an absolutely gorgeous day, and I shielded my eyes with my hand, watching for him to come up for air. Right on time, his head popped up a few minutes later. Then back down he went. I felt happy, knowing he was having fun. A short while later, there he was again, popping up through the water, now in the center of the lagoon.

A lot of kids were out on the swimming dock. I watched them jumping off, playing around with each other, pretending to push one another toward the edge. They were laughing and splashing and obviously having a good time.

The sun was warm, and the water was rippling ever so slightly in the soft, tropical breeze. *What a wonderful place this is,* I thought, gazing at the picturesque houses that dotted the hillside surrounding the lagoon. Here and there a big splash of colorful blossoms seemed to burst out from under the thick foliage. Along some parts of the lagoon, trees went right down to the water. Along other sections, houses stood along the water's edge; boats bobbed in little docks connected to the houses with rambling little catwalks.

I jumped, suddenly aware of the passage of time. I looked at my watch, frowning as I studied its face and calculated how long it had been since I'd seen Trent. He'd gone into the water about 2:00. Now it was nearly 2:30. I scanned the lagoon, watching for Trent's head to pop through the surface again.

I couldn't see him. I stood up, hoping to have a better view. I knew he was out there; I just couldn't see him. Another ten minutes went by.

A boat came into the cove, and again I was distracted, fretting that it was going right over the top of the lagoon, making it difficult for me to see. It wasn't going very fast, but I couldn't help thinking, *They shouldn't let boats go over the lagoon. There are people swimming in there. Trent will have something to say about that, I'll bet.*

And then Trent's words from a few days before flashed through my memory, his telling me about how sounds are deceiving when you're underwater, and I thought, *Trent! I hope you hear the boat! I hope you hear it! I hope you're OK!*

Another fifteen minutes passed. Now I was walking anxiously along the edge of the dock, peering out toward the lagoon. When the boat came in to the dock, I trotted over a catwalk and hurried out onto another dock to meet it. I will never forget the feeling that swept over me at that moment: *If I say what I'm afraid of, it will become real, and I don't want it to be real—not at all.*

I wanted to scream, but instead I said simply, "My husband's out there, and I can't see him." The two men in the boat looked up at me curiously. "He's free diving; he was supposed to be back in fifteen minutes, and it's been—it's been nearly forty-five minutes." I wasn't crying, but there was no way I could keep the panicky tremor from rising into my voice. "Would you take me out there?" I asked the strangers. "Would you take me to look for him?"

"Of course. Get in," the boat's driver said.

We cruised slowly over to the lagoon and peered down into its mysterious depths. The water was crystal clear; we could see quite a way down. But there was no sign of Trent. We drove all around the lagoon and then moved outward, looking among the trees and foliage along the edge. Then we went back to the hole and circled it again.

Nothing.

The men took me back to the dock. One of them said to me gently, "He must be OK, because if anything had happened to him . . . he would float up to the top." I looked at him in shock, and when I stepped off the boat, I broke down, sobbing in absolute fear. I didn't know what to do. Trent was in there; he was in that hole. I knew it.

I wanted to believe what the man had said, that if something had gone wrong, if the unthinkable had happened, Trent's body would float to the top. But then another needlelike thought spiked my brain: *Trent was diving with weights on, so if something happened, he wouldn't float. He would sink. He wouldn't come up.*

SEARCHING FOR TRENT

I hurried off the dock and asked everyone around, "Do you have any masks? Do you have a snorkel? Do you have anything I can borrow? Because my husband's out there, and I have to go find him."

"Ma'am—what? What's happened?" a man said, surprised by my tears and my sobbing pleas.

"My husband went free diving in the lagoon, and he didn't come back. We went out in the boat, but we couldn't see him. But I know he's out there, and I have to find him!"

"You're probably the wrong person to go out there right now," the man said, putting a hand on my arm. "You just hang on."

"Then can we please call a dive team?" I said, starting to sob now.

I followed him inside and heard him make the phone call, then I went back outside to wait. Nervously I walked along the edge of the docks, my eyes constantly on the water, my heart praying steadily, *Oh, dear God. Oh, dear Jesus. Help me. Help Trent. Save him.*

12

Father God

I'm O.K., yes I am. Somebody hold me.
Here I am, here I am. Lord, I need you now.

I love you, I love you,
I love you, Father God, Father God.
I need you, I need you,
I need you, Father God, Father God.

I still believe with my hands lifted high,
Even though I ask the questions why,
Even though my heart, it still cries,
Oh, oh, I still believe.
My heart, it longs to be free.
I'm here, I'm here, oh, yes!

—Tammy Trent & Pete Orta

12 | waiting

IT TOOK THIRTY TO FORTY MINUTES for the dive team to arrive. I watched the men pull on their gear and swim out to the lagoon. Then they too were gone.

I waited at the restaurant where we had eaten lunch, my mind aching with the thought that something was terribly, terribly wrong. I wandered out onto the restaurant's open-air dining room; now another couple was eating at the table Trent and I had shared. They glanced up at me as I paced along the railing, constantly looking out to the lagoon. As I turned, our eyes met for a moment, and I saw the surprise on their faces as they read the shock and fear on mine. They were obviously thinking, *Look at that poor girl. Something's wrong.*

I went inside and asked to use the telephone. The staff didn't know what to do with me, a distraught customer who paced around the place, probably scaring away customers. Now they quickly jumped at the chance to do something for me. The manager kindly led me into the restaurant's office and pointed to the phone on the desk.

I dropped slowly into the chair and pulled the phone toward me. My hand trembled as I punched in the numbers to call Trent's parents.

When she heard my voice, Mom Lenderink knew immediately this wasn't a normal call. "What's wrong?" she asked.

"I can't find Trent," I said, my voice wavering up and down the scale. "I can't find him."

"What do you mean?" she asked.

"He went diving, and he hasn't come back, and I can't find him. I've searched for him, and I can't find him. Something's wrong."

She said, "Are you sure?"

"Yes. I *know* something's wrong," I sobbed. I told her about searching the lagoon with the two men in the boat. I told her a dive team was in the water.

She said, "Honey, let me get off the phone and call Dad. He's on a business trip. Let me call Tom."

I told her the number of the restaurant and then hung up. Moments later, Dad Lenderink called. He said, "Tammy, what's happened? What's going on?"

"Dad, Trent went into the water. He went free diving. He said he'd be back in fifteen minutes, and he hasn't come back, and it's been more than an hour."

Trent's dad said, "Tammy, he's probably OK. You know, he's been diving so long. He knows what he's doing. He probably just got interested in something and forgot about the time. I really think he's probably OK. Just give it some time. I think everything will be OK."

"No, Dad, really. I know something's wrong."

He said, "Let me get off the phone; I need to call Mom." He was very calm as he said good-bye. I wanted him to be right. I wanted everything to be OK. But I knew it wasn't.

Next I called my mom, but she wasn't home. I left a message on her answering machine: "Mom, I need you to pray for me. Pray for Trent, Mom. I can't find him, and I don't know what to do."

I left the same tearful message on Gina's answering machine. Then Mom Lenderink called me back and said, "Dad is going to try to get to you, but he's in Los Angeles, and I don't know when he can get a flight." I was relieved to know he realized the seriousness of the situation and felt reassured that he believed me now—although I understood why he wouldn't do so initially. We all knew Trent was an adventurer, and we knew he was a really smart guy. We believed he could get himself out of any predicament. If he was stuck someplace, hung up on some coral or something, he would figure out a way to escape. We had no doubt about that. Something like this would not happen to Trent. He wouldn't go diving and not come back. Not Trent.

REFLEX ACTION

I sat in that office, so thankful the restaurant manager was allowing me to completely take over the phone. Trent had taken his cell phone with us to Jamaica, but it was absolutely useless there. He had tried several times during the week to use it, but he wasn't able to get service at all. The restaurant manager's name was Matthew; he was the owner's son. They were Americans. Matthew kept easing quietly into the office to check on me.

"You've gotta hang on, Tammy," he would say. "There's still hope. There's still a possibility." And sometimes he would say, "I'm so sorry, Tammy. I'm so sorry you're going through this. Do you need something? Could I get you some water?" Most importantly at that moment, he told me, "Use the phone. Call whoever you want to call."

Then Matthew's mom came in; her name was Valerie, and she owned the restaurant. She was a precious, beautiful lady who held me and hugged me as I cried. When she stepped out of the office, I tried again to reach someone back home, someone who could pray with me, reassure me, and help me through this awful nightmare. But all I could do was leave messages. No one was home.

My thoughts plunged me into even greater despair: *Trent saved me my whole life, and now I'm sitting here and I can't save him. I can't save you, Trent. I don't know what to do, and I'm so sorry. I don't know what to do. If I were as smart as you, I could figure this out. You always know what to do. You can figure out anything. But I don't know what to do. I don't know what you want me to do, Trent. What am I supposed to do?*

I sat there with tears racing down my face, and all I could do at that moment, being so numb, so shocked, so scared, was to lift up my hands toward heaven. It was an automatic reflex. I thought later that it was like the response of a soldier who's so thoroughly trained in what to do when he's thrown into combat that, even though he's terrified, he responds automatically. He has practiced for that possibility for so long that his body responds even though his mind is too numb to think. That's where I was at that moment. I could no longer think for myself. I was helpless. But there was a part of me that had practiced for this moment my whole life, and that part took over. So, sitting there alone in that room, I lifted my hands and my heart toward heaven and begged, *Jesus, help me. God, help me. I don't know what to do. Save me, dear Jesus. I'm not so good at asking for help, but I need you to help me now. I don't know what to do.*

I had collapsed onto the floor, dropping down between the desk and the chair, and now I arose to pace the floor. And as I walked back and forth across the room, another automatic response began. I closed my eyes and started to sing: "I love you, Lord, and I lift my voice . . . to worship you. Oh my soul, rejoice. Take joy, my king, in what you hear . . ."

I was so broken I could barely get the words out, but still, they came, lyrics I had written or recorded or sung a thousand times:

"You're shaken up, you're breaking down with the weight of problems . . . You're all but lost . . . Hope can't be found in the place your heart is . . . So bewildered and confused, you've done all that you can do . . . We rely upon ourselves until we're standing on the brink . . . Sometimes the hardest thing to do is just give up, when you don't have the strength."

When I opened my eyes, Valerie had slipped back into the room and was sitting in a chair beside another woman. It probably was a very strange thing for them, seeing this distraught woman pacing the room, singing, of all things, praise songs. But I was on autopilot, and at that moment in that hard situation, that's all I knew to do. The words that came to me were lyrics that had everything to do with my life at that exact moment, and they flowed out of me like a lifeline tying me to hope:

"You're the hope that I have inside . . . You're the joy that has changed my life . . . You're the passion that fills my soul, and a peace like I've never known . . . It's wonderful believing; you never let me go . . . You are the heart of me. You are the breath I breathe, my all, my everything . . . My Irreplaceable."

The other woman who had come in with Valerie was a doctor she had called. She offered something to calm me down, but I wasn't ready to take anything.

The phone rang again, and Valerie nodded for me to answer it. It was my mom. She was in Marion, Illinois, doing a ministry share-a-thon on Christian television. Her husband, Keith, had gotten my message and called her. "Tammy? Honey, are you all right?"

"Mom! Oh, Mom!" The tears flowed again. My mom's voice was the one I needed to hear, but even more, I longed to feel her arms around me, comforting me in the way only a mother can do.

"Oh, baby, I want to be there for you," she said. "I don't think I can get a flight this late in the day, but I'm going to try. I'll get there, honey. I'll get there." And then she prayed, "Oh, Jesus, send somebody for my little girl. We ask in Jesus' name that you bring Trent back to her. Oh, Father . . ."

Pam Thum called, and she also prayed with me. "Tammy, we're just praying that he's stuck somewhere . . . that he's found an air pocket, and he's OK. He'll find a way to come back to you."

My Mom and Pam were praying for Trent to come back to me. I wanted to share their hope, cling to the same kind of faith they had. But I was the one sitting there beside that lagoon, knowing he was gone.

The sun had set, and the dive team came back. "We've got to stop for the night," one of them told me. "We don't have enough light to see anything. But we'll be back in the morning." He told me they had gone all the way to the bottom of the hole, 240 feet, and they had looked along the edges of the lagoon. They hadn't found any sign of Trent, but tomorrow they would look again.

Now I took the Valium the doctor offered me. I was caught between reality and an unbelievable nightmare, thinking, *This isn't happening. If I scream, then it means it's happening. If I yell at God, that means it's happening. If I cry real hard, it means it's happening. So I'm not screaming. I'm not yelling. I'm holding in the tears as much as I can, and that means this isn't happening.*

Valerie offered me some pieces of fruit she had cut up. I tried to eat but couldn't. The doctor was still there, and now her husband joined us. He was a physician too. Everyone was treating me with the greatest kindness, patting me, soothing me, trying to offer comfort. They asked me where I was staying, and I answered, "We were supposed to be in Kingston tonight, but I want to stay here instead. Could I just sleep on the dock?"

There were no hotels anywhere around; we were in the middle of nowhere. "I'm staying here until we find Trent," I said. "If you'll let me, I'll sleep on the dock."

"Oh, no, honey. You can't sleep here," Valerie said. "You can come home with me." I knew, for my safety, she didn't want me sleeping there. And also, I think they all thought it would be best if I wasn't anywhere near the dock in case they recovered Trent's body. They didn't want me to see it.

Then one of the doctors said to Valerie, "I think it would be better if she stays with us. Then we can keep an eye on her and make sure she's all right."

I think they were concerned that Valerie would smother me with too much attention, but I didn't know that at the time. I was too out of it to care. Looking back on it, I think that was the wrong choice, because Valerie was extending the kind of care and comfort I needed right then—a mother's loving concern. But the two doctors were kind enough to offer their home, and I was in no position to argue.

THE LONG, LONG NIGHT

Their home was about a mile away, up a long road that wound through what looked like a jungle. The wife drove me up there, and there were no lights anywhere around as we approached the A-frame house; it was very dark. She parked the car, looked over at me, and said encouragingly, "You're doing really well."

"Am I?" I asked, amazed that she would say so.

"Yes," she answered, "you're doing very well."

She showed me to the bedroom where I would sleep, but before I settled in I realized I had some commitments I needed to tend to. We were supposed to be in Kingston the next day to begin the mission trip, and I had no idea who to call. I dug through Trent's paperwork, and all I could find was a Nashville number for Salem Communications. It was late, and I had to leave a message in voice mail: "This is Tammy, and something's happened, and I won't be there in Kingston tomorrow. I can't find Trent, and I don't know who to call. So could you please let the people in Kingston know we won't be there?"

Then I realized I also had a big booking just a few days later back in the States. So once more I dug through Trent's papers until I found the number for the choreographer, and I left the same message: "Something's happened. I won't be coming. Please let the dancers know and contact the festival organizers for me."

Next I called my good friends Pete and Kelli Orta in Nashville, and Kelli asked if I wanted her to call our pastors there. We had been attending Bethel World Outreach, but we weren't officially members. I told Kelli, "Yes, please call them, even though they probably don't know me. I would appreciate their prayers."

Within ten minutes, Pastors Rice Broocks and Tim Johnson from Bethel called me; they were both on the phone at once, and their words were so comforting to me. We talked and prayed together before saying good-bye.

Then I thought I might be able to sleep. But the doctors' house had no air conditioning, and it felt like the temperature was about ninety degrees. When she had brought me to the room where I would sleep, the wife-doctor said, "We'll open up the windows so you'll get some ventilation through here. But you'll probably have critters coming in through the night. So you'll need to drop the mosquito netting."

Over the bed, a circular rod held long veils of netting that would enclose the bed. Wondering just what kind of "critters" might be interested in visiting, I got ready for bed and then made some more phone calls. Dad Lenderink, Pam Thum, Mom, Norm, Gina and her husband, Ken—all of them told me they had made flight arrangements and would be flying to Jamaica tomorrow to join me. All I had to do was get through the night, and they would be here tomorrow. I was reassured, knowing they were coming.

But I didn't know—nobody knew—that tomorrow the whole world would change.

Because tomorrow would be September 11, 2001.

13

Blessed are those who mourn,
for they will be comforted.

—Matthew 5:4

13 | the day the world changed

I LIFTED THE MOSQUITO NETTING and crawled into bed, but I was so hot, so uncomfortable, I couldn't sleep. I got up and tiptoed out into the main room, found the switch for the ceiling fan, and turned it on. Then I lay down on the couch.

I heard a car coming up the hill, and I thought. *It's Trent! That car's going to stop at this house, and Trent's going to get out. I just know that's who's in that car.*

The car did stop at the house, and I sat up on the couch, holding my breath. The door opened. *Oh, God, please* . . . But it was the doctor, the husband, apparently returning from a late-night call. He came in the door and didn't see me on the couch since the lights were out. He walked into the other bedroom and closed the door.

After a while I walked through the sliding doors at one end of the main room and stepped onto the deck; I gasped at the view. It was so very dark, but a huge dome of brilliant stars spanned the sky. Down below, moonlight sparkled on the water. It was breathtakingly beautiful. But standing there, looking at the spectacular expanse, I lost it, realizing that Trent was somewhere down there. Now my fear became, *If he's not alive, what if he's swept out into the ocean and we never find him?*

Earlier that night I had told my close friend Pete Orta that I could never come back without Trent. "If we don't find him, I'll never come home, Pete. So we have to find him. Please, Pete, pray that we find him, because I don't think I could ever leave without him."

I knew I would never have closure in my life if we didn't find Trent's body.

Lying down again, I fell into a fitful sleep. The next thing I knew, I was standing on the balcony once more, looking out over the dark water sparkling in the moonlight. Something was rustling the foliage below the deck. The palms and shrubs were moving and swaying as though something was pushing its way through them, climbing up the hill. Then the thing emerged from the edge of the greenery.

It was Trent.

Ohhhhhh. Thank God! Thank you, Jesus! I prayed.

Trent climbed up onto the deck and took me in his arms. Oh, the relief I felt!

"Tammy, baby! I'm so sorry, I'm so sorry, I'm so sorry," he said, all in a rush. "I didn't mean to scare you, but I got stuck, and then everybody was gone and I couldn't find my way back. When I finally got back to the dock, they told me you were up here. I took a shortcut through the trees; I wanted to get to you as fast I could. I knew how upset you would be. I'm so sorry, baby." The words flowed out of him like an unstoppable flood.

"Trent! Don't *ever* scare me like that again!" I sobbed into his shoulder. "Oh, Trent! I thought I had lost you! It was just a dream, but it felt so real."

The feeling I had at that moment was pure euphoria; I wanted to cling to Trent and never let him go. But it was just a tear-drenched pillow I was clinging to, not Trent. I was dreaming, and the voice of the husband-doctor awakened me. There was a strange edge in the sound of his voice. "Tammy, you ought to come and look at this," he said. "Something's happened in America."

I could tell it was CNN by the tape of words marching steadily across the bottom of the screen. Next I recognized that it was broadcasting pictures of the World Trade Center's twin towers in New York City. Huge mushrooms of ugly, black smoke billowed furiously out of the side of one of the towers, and as I watched, unbelieving, an airplane zipped in from the edge of the screen, plowed into the second tower, and vanished.

I held my breath, waiting for the next step. It was obvious to me that the world was ending, and now we were all going to heaven. *We're next. We're going. I'll see Trent. It's happening. It's really happening.*

I was ready.

The moment passed, the misery continued, and the world didn't end. But in that instant it had changed forever, just as my own personal world had changed the day before.

"HAVE YOU FOUND HIM?"

Not knowing anything else to do, I called down to the dock. "Have you found him?" I asked. "What's happening down there? Is the dive team there? I want to come down there. Will you come get me?"

Yes, I was told, the dive team was in the water, but no, Trent hadn't been found, and no, it wasn't a good idea for me to come down there. Just wait there, the man at the dock told me. It will be better if you wait up there.

As I hung up the phone, the husband-doctor motioned for me to join him at the kitchen table. "Tammy, I just want to warn you of a couple things and just prepare you," he said. "If you do see Trent, if they do recover his body, he may not look the same."

I could only look at him, the tears rolling again; I was unable to speak. "There are fish and crabs in the water, Tammy, you know, and they . . . pick at . . . they eat . . ."

He looked straight at me, trying to determine if I was understanding what he was telling me. I was stunned that he would say such things, yet I also knew it was his way of trying to prepare me for the worst. Trent had been down in that hole all night, nearly twenty-four hours, and now the doctor was saying, "He's probably not going to look very good, you know, with those creatures down there . . ."

I have no idea how many times I called the dock that morning, but it was a lot. I don't remember the person answering the phone ever showing impatience or weariness at my repeated questions. Always, his answer was the same: nothing yet.

Looking back, I know I was one of thousands of people that morning, calling and waiting, desperately seeking information about loved ones. The difference at that point was that in New York and Washington, D.C., and in towns and cities all across America, those families were waiting with hope. But for me, hope had run out.

SO ALONE . . .

My brother called. "Tammy, they've grounded all the planes. Mom and Gina and Ken . . . everyone's trying to get to you, but nothing is flying," he said.

Never had I felt so isolated, so alone, as I did listening to his words. "So nobody's coming?" I asked. "Nobody can get to me?"

"They're trying, Tammy," Norm said. "But it doesn't look good."

"Norm, explain it to me. What is going on? What's happening? I don't understand."

Norm told me as much as he knew about the tragedies that had occurred that morning. I hung up the phone, reeling from this additional blow, overwhelmed by what was happening in my world—and in the rest of the world too.

Then Trent's sister Tracey called from Michigan. Sobs interrupting her words, she cried into the phone, "Tammy, they've found Trent! They've found his body."

I couldn't believe what I was hearing. "No, Tracey, they haven't. I haven't gotten that call," I told her. "I just talked to the guy at the dock, and they have not found Trent."

She said, "Well, somebody called us. Who would have called us and told us such a thing?"

"I don't know, but nobody's called me, so I don't think they've found him."

I hung up and immediately called the dock again. "No," the man said, probably for the twentieth time, "they haven't found him yet."

Numb and confused, I sat on the couch, holding my head in my hands. Across the room, the television was showing pictures of a huge wall of dust sweeping down New York streets. Then the scene jumped to an aerial view of the Pentagon; smoke billowed up from there too. The words crawling across the bottom of the screen described an airplane crash somewhere in Pennsylvania. I saw these things, I heard them, but nothing registered in my mind. I was locked inside my own solitary world of grief and fear.

The phone rang again, and the doctor-husband picked it up in the office toward the back of the house. I heard him speak softly into the phone, then he stepped back into the main room. I listened, hoping he wasn't coming to tell me what I knew he *was* going to tell me. "Tammy," he said softly, "they found Trent. They found him in the hole."

I melted onto the floor, buried my face in the carpet, pounded my fist and finally let out all the pent-up terror and grief and pain. "What happened?" That's all I could say, over and over again, as I wailed and moaned. "What happened? What went wrong? What happened? Jesus, what happened? Trent, what happened? Trent, baby, what happened? What went wrong?" I couldn't stop crying, and for half an hour, the doctors left me there on the floor to mourn in loud, agonizing solitude. They probably realized it was useless to try and console me. I was beyond their reach emotionally.

Finally, still trembling but back in control, I managed to get up off the floor and stand. There were more phone calls to be made now.

Just as I dialed the first number, Trent's dad walked in the door.

14

This is the end of the world.
This is Armageddon.

—My sister, Gina, on September 11, 2001,
learning of the terrorist attacks
while onboard a grounded flight.

14 | grounded

OR MY FAMILY AND ME, September 11 will always be a harsh reminder, not only of the murderous terrorist attacks on our country, but also for our own personal nightmare that was unfolding in our lives. In this chapter, I've asked some of them to share how they endured that bewildering and grief-filled time.

GINA: *Life, As We Know It, Will Never Be the Same*

Monday, September 10, was a beautiful day in Chicago. While Kenny and Kyle played on the swing set in our backyard, I sat in the sunshine, singing and playing my guitar. I ran inside when I heard the phone, but when the caller ID said "out of area," I assumed it was a telemarketer and let the machine answer it. Without waiting to listen, I went back outside to enjoy the beautiful late afternoon with the boys.

Later, when we came in, I played the message and smiled when I heard Tammy's voice. So many times in the past Tammy, Trent, Ken, and I had left silly little messages to make each other laugh, and for an instant, I thought this was one of those calls. Then I heard the panic in Tammy's voice, and my smile evaporated.

Tammy said Trent had been free diving, and he didn't come up and she couldn't find him. I didn't even wait for the rest of the message. I picked up the phone and dialed her cell phone. Frustrated to hear the busy tone, I dialed over and over again, my fingers shaking uncontrollably and my prayers spilling out in a jumble: "a miracle Lord, a miracle, Lord, I pray for a miracle. No, no, no, no, no, this can't be happening, not to Trent. Oh Jesus, oh Jesus, please."

After fifteen minutes of this futile redialing, I called a close friend and asked her to get a prayer chain started within our church. Then I called Ken at work, but the call went into his voice mail. So I called our friend Omar, who works with Ken and who knew Trent and Tammy. When I explained why I was calling, he hurried to locate Ken, eventually finding him in the workout facility in another building. He rushed into the gym, handed Ken his cell phone, and said, "Something's happened to Trent."

Ken rushed home. While I made arrangements for the boys to stay with family friends, Ken located our passports and booked flights for Tuesday morning.

Since I hadn't listened to all of Tammy's message, I didn't even know where we were going once we got to Jamaica. I called Trent's mom to get the details and was reassured by how calm she was. "I'm sure everything's going to be OK," she said, but she added that Trent's dad was flying to Jamaica too.

When I hung up, the phone rang again, and it was Tammy. "Gina," she cried, "I've lost Trent! I've lost Trent, Gina, and I . . . I feel like I can't breathe, Gina. I don't know what to do."

"Calm down, Tammy. Take deep breaths," I told her. We breathed together for a while, but the truth was that I felt panicky too. It was unbearable to be so far apart when she needed me so badly. I just wanted to hold her, to cry with her, to pray with her. "We're coming, Tammy," I told her. "Our flight leaves tomorrow morning; we'll be there as soon as we can. Mom and Keith are coming too. Hang on, Tammy. We'll be there tomorrow."

Mom's husband, Keith, flew in from Grand Rapids and met us at the airport in Chicago Tuesday morning. Mom was catching a flight out of St. Louis and would meet us when we changed planes in Miami. Then we would all fly together to Jamaica. As we hurried down the concourse,

I envisioned us all arriving in Jamaica and finding Trent and Tammy waiting. We would have a big feast, I imagined, to celebrate Trent's narrow escape, and all of us would tell Trent how scared we were, thinking something had happened to him.

I seriously believed he was OK, because we all knew Trent could get out of any situation. Then, as we boarded the plane, I looked at my watch and realized it had been fourteen hours since Trent had gone into the water . . .

The plane taxied away from the gate; we lumbered along and finally felt the big jet turn onto the runway. The engines accelerated for takeoff, and I reached for Ken's hand, relieved to know we were finally on our way to Tammy. But just as the plane should have started forward, the huge engines died down again, and instead of roaring off down the runway, the plane started taxiing again and eventually pulled off onto the tarmac.

Inside the plane, everything was totally silent. For forty-five minutes we heard nothing from the cockpit. I looked out the window and tugged on Ken's sleeve. "Honey, look at all the other planes. Everyone's parked. Not one plane is moving," I told him.

Despite the rules banning cell phone use after the plane's doors were shut, people started making calls. Ken called Omar and asked what was happening. A plane had just flown into one of the twin towers, he said, and while he and Ken were talking, Omar was watching TV and gasped in astonishment as another plane hit the second tower.

Ken relayed to me what Omar was telling him. Then he shook his head, stunned by the news. "Life, as we know it, will never be the same," he said.

Ken asked Omar to call Tammy and let her know we wouldn't be able to get to her. Then he hung up. But in just a few minutes, the cell phone rang, and it was Omar, calling us back. Ken listened a moment, then said quietly, "OK. Thank you, Omar."

Ken turned back to me and reached for my hand. "They found Trent," he said.

"Alive?" I asked him, holding my breath.

"No. They pulled him out of the water."

I cried out so loudly that a flight attendant came hurrying down the aisle to check on me. She was crying too. She told us later that her friends had been working one of the hijacked flights. I thought, *This is the end of the world. This must be Armageddon.*

PAM THUM: *An Inexcplicable Sadness*

I had just finished singing at a women's conference in Canada, and the women and I were laughing and hugging, joyful in our time together, when I felt an inexplicable sadness, a lonely feeling that made me want to cry. It was such a strange, unexpected feeling in that happy setting. Then, a few hours later, the message arrived: "Call Tammy. Urgent."

I dialed the number on the message and cried when I heard Tammy sob on the other end of the line. "I can't find Trent," she said. "The divers are looking for him."

"Tammy, hon, he probably got out of the water and is off exploring somewhere," I told her. I was pushing so hard to believe what I was telling her, but Tammy knew better.

"Pam, I can feel that he's gone," Tammy cried. "I think I've lost my boy."

"Tammy, I'll be there as soon as I can," I promised.

I hung up and called Steve, my husband. We live in the same Nashville neighborhood as Tammy and Trent, and we have been best friends forever. I could hear Steve's usually rock-solid voice shake as he told me, "Trent will be OK. He's probably just out looking around. He *can't* be gone, Pam. Not Trent."

Two hours later, I spoke to Tammy again. Now she was at the doctors' house, and she was sobbing softly, obviously exhausted. She sounded like a lost little girl. We prayed together, softly telling Jesus we loved him. I whispered over and over to Tammy, "Peace, peace, peace."

She was lying on the bed as we spoke, and I told her, "Tammy, your mom and Gina and I are right there with you on that bed. We are cuddling with you. Your mom is stroking your hair, and Gina and I are rubbing your back and your feet. We are there right now with you. Take a deep breath. Keep breathing, Tammy, and feel us there with you. Feel the angels in the room with you; they are singing to you and holding you too."

My plan was to catch an early flight out of Buffalo on Tuesday morning. I would meet Steve back in Nashville, and we would leave immediately for Jamaica. But before I left for the airport, my cell phone rang again. It was Steve, but I could hardly understand him. He seemed to be choking on the words. "They found Trent's body, Pam," he said. "He's gone. He's gone."

I crumpled onto the floor and screamed at the top of my lungs, "No! No! No!" My sister-in-law and brother-in-law heard my cries and came running to comfort me. But I cried all the harder, realizing I had someone to hold me, but my dear Tammy, so far away, was weeping all alone. *Oh, Jesus! Hold her now!* I begged.

Eventually I pulled myself together and headed to the airport. Walking to my gate, I passed a group of people staring wide-eyed at a TV monitor. It looked as if an airplane had hit one of the twin towers in New York City. As I moved down the jet bridge to board the plane, I prayed aloud for the ones involved in that tragedy: "Dear Jesus, comfort those people and heal them."

I settled into my seat and closed my eyes, exhausted. But a few moments later, the captain's solemn voice announced that "all flights have been grounded. Please exit the aircraft."

The airport was in a frenzy. People were obviously dazed. Others seemed to not know where they were. Fear and uncertainty filled every eye. Like everyone else, I stood in the concourse, not knowing exactly what to do but whispering, "Jesus . . . Jesus . . . Jesus." Tears rolled down my face, but slowly a wonderful sense of peace swept over me. My shoulders went back, and my head went up. I could almost feel Jesus holding me, lifting me up so securely I felt like I was on my tiptoes. It was an awesome experience. I felt enveloped by this one stunning thought: *Trent went to heaven, and the whole world shifted.*

MOM: *Finding God's Grace in the Most Painful Situations*

When I think back on that experience, as difficult as it was, I'm amazed by how God sends his grace in the most painful and frightening situations. In the hours following Tammy's call with the news that Trent was missing, peace filled my mind as I thought of the healing that had occurred just weeks earlier between Tammy's dad and me. Trent's passion for life and love was responsible. When he invited Keith and me, as well as my ex-husband, Norm, and his wife, Val, to join him and Tammy for dinner on their anniversary, it was the first time in twenty-five years I had sat at a table with Norm. The walls came down that night, and we laughed and enjoyed our time together. When we parted, we all hugged and wished each other well. I felt a great warmth, understanding then that forgiveness is the best medicine in the world.

Unable to get a flight out of St. Louis on the night Tammy called, I had booked a seat on an early morning flight the next day. I called Norm on my way to the airport, but as soon as I heard his voice, I began to cry. "Do you know?" I managed to ask.

Through a tear-shaken voice, he said, "Yes." He paused to regain control, then he said, "Jude, go take care of our little girl."

"I'm on my way," I told him.

And then 9/11 happened. The terror in the airport was chilling, and people were panicked. My thoughts flew to my kids. *Please, God, please be with them. Hold Trent. Hold Tammy. Please, Jesus.*

There were no rental cars left at the airport. But by a miracle, a friend showed up out of nowhere and took me to a rental agency off the airport grounds. I drove to Chicago, where Keith was waiting with Gina and Ken. While driving, I called Norm and Val again, hoping to hear that Trent had been found and that he was OK. But as soon as Val answered the phone, she cried, "Judy, they found Trent. He's gone."

"No! No! No! My God, not Trent!" I don't know how long I screamed, gripping the steering wheel so fiercely it probably bent. I had dropped my cell phone onto the seat, but I still could hear Norm's voice calling loudly, "Jude! Stop the car! Pull over! Jude, please, we don't need another tragedy."

I pulled to the side of the road to regain my composure, then I finished the drive, falling into Gina's arms when I got to her house. My baby girl became a pillar of strength for all of us, and I was comforted to know that the one I used to hold was now holding me and wiping my tears away. But as we cried together, I thought, *Who's holding Tammy? Oh, Jesus, how can she bear this alone?*

Then the Holy Spirit reminded me of Jesus's promise to Tammy—and to all of us: "I will never leave you or forsake you." And, "I will send you a comforter."

Keith and I, along with Ken, Gina, and their boys, drove home to Grand Rapids to wait for Tammy to bring Trent home. Surprisingly, during that time, Norm, Val, Keith, and I found comfort in each other. We couldn't have done that if Trent hadn't brought us together again. Norm and Val would come over to have dinner with all of us. We would call Tammy in Jamaica and share our love and support for her.

One night she told me, "Mom, I just wanna die. How am I ever gonna live without Trent? I can't breathe, Mom!"

I answered quickly, "Trent wants you to breathe, honey. He wants you to live. Now, take a deep breath. You've got to keep breathing."

TRENT'S MOM: *Praying for Trent to Call*

After Tammy called with the awful news about Trent, I immediately called my husband, Tom, and our son Troy; they were in Los Angeles on business. I interrupted their meeting and told Tom he had to get on a flight immediately. He at first questioned whether there could really be a problem; we all knew Trent was so capable and dependable. But Tom honored my desperate-mother wishes and booked a seat on the last flight to Jamaica that evening.

Tom arrived in Kingston without a passport or any of the necessary credentials, but Valerie, the owner of the restaurant at the Blue Lagoon, had sent a friend to meet him, and they walked through all the immigration points that morning without anyone ever asking for a thing! Perhaps everyone was in shock due to the bombings that occurred in the U.S. just as Tom arrived. But to him, it seemed that an angel had gone before him to clear the way.

Back home, our family immediately gathered after Tammy called, and we prayed most of the night. Finally I went to bed and tried to sleep, the cordless phone next to me, praying that any minute it would ring, and I would hear Trent's voice telling me everything was OK.

The next morning, Tom called to let us know he had made it to

Kingston. Then, with all the family gathered together, we heard of the terrorist bombings just as I received another phone call. It was the call that told us Trent's body had been found. I fell to the floor, sobbing.

The rest of the day was a blur. It seemed impossible to grasp the enormity of what had happened: realizing I had lost Trent and seeing all the tragedy unfolding on the television. At that point I was just like the people who had lost family in the bombings, but it was as if my pain wasn't recognized. I hurt, hearing the reporters talk so much about the horrible grief of the spouses but forgetting that the mothers and fathers were also going through tremendous pain as well.

The next few days brought such an onslaught of flowers to our home that florists sometimes called and said they had an order for flowers but didn't have enough to send. They were running out!

Our son Tate hired a friend to bring meals to us for several weeks; we had at least twenty people here for dinner every night. Many friends shared our grief and the grief of the nation, and being together helped us heal.

15

So bless GOD, you angels,
  ready and able to fly at his bidding,
  quick to hear and do what he says.

  —*Psalm 103:20* MSG

15 | the angel

O N MONDAY, when I had called our families back in the States, Dad Lenderink had been the one who had seemed the least convinced that something serious had happened to Trent. Yet he was the one who had immediately gotten on a plane and made his way to me.

Mom Lenderink wrote to me later, saying, "I imagine that your father-in-law was the last one you would have wanted to be with you at that difficult time. I know you longed for your mother's arms and your sister's comforting presence. But looking back, I believe Tom was the only one who could have done what had to be done. And Tammy, if your mother or Gina or Pam had made it, you might have relied on their strength and not on God's. Then you might not have glimpsed that angel who came to you there."

She was right. Of all the family members I might have wanted to be with me at that time, Dad Lenderink probably would not have been first on my list. I love and appreciate him, but in that heartbreaking situation, I longed for the kindred compassion of Mom, Gina, and Pam, the women I'm closest to. Looking back, however, I see that Dad Lenderink was the only one who could have done what had to be done in the next few days. Difficult, heartbreaking, infuriating steps lay ahead of us before we could take Trent's body back to America. I was blessed to have

Dad Lenderink there to help me with his strength, patience, and level-headed way of communicating.

When he walked through the door of the doctors' house that day, I dropped the phone and rushed to him, collapsing into his arms. He made his way to the couch, and I eased onto the floor beside him, clinging to his legs. He patted my shoulders as I sobbed.

Like me, he wanted to find out exactly what had happened. When I finally regained control of myself, he went into the other room to make some calls and try to get more information. When he came back into the room, his face was grim. "Tammy, they've taken Trent's body to the morgue, and it has to be formally identified. We need to go. Do you feel up to it?"

I nodded yes.

Matthew, Valerie's son, who had been so kind to me at the restaurant the day before, volunteered to drive us to the morgue, about forty-five minutes away. It was a harsh, unfriendly place; the employees we dealt with seemed emotionless—uncaring and unfeeling. Matthew went with us to the front desk and explained who we were. The receptionist never smiled, never expressed condolences. She just told us to wait. We were Americans in a foreign country, and the people who ran the morgue were strictly business. There was apparently no room for compassion.

We had to wait quite awhile, then someone came and got us. "OK, you can come in," he said sternly. Matthew waited in the lobby; Dad Lenderink and I walked resolutely down the hall.

MY BEAUTIFUL TRENT

As we walked into the room, two attendants were wheeling a table through another set of doors. On the table was a body covered with a sheet. *Trent's body.* We watched as they pushed the gurney into the center of the room. Then one of them pulled back the sheet, and there was Trent.

He lay there in that familiar dive suit, and he looked so perfect, as though he were sleeping. Unstoppable tears flowed down my cheeks and dropped onto his face as I leaned down to him and whispered desperately,

"Can you just wake up, Trent? Can you just wake up? You're right there; you're lying there. Can you just wake up?"

He looked beautiful, perfect. Apparently, no creatures had touched him. There wasn't a single scratch on his face. I touched his leg, and it felt soft and surprisingly warm. I kissed his face once, and then again. It too felt soft and surprisingly warm. He looked so handsome, so perfect. Even his hair was just right, spiked up a bit in just the right place and lying smooth against his head everywhere else. Then I noticed a little line of blood coming from his ear; it had dripped onto the paper covering the table. That bothered me, seeing the blood on Trent. I felt my legs start to tremble, and black splotches filled my vision. Dad, feeling me sway, tightened his grip on my arm and held me up.

In a moment I nodded that I was OK, and he released my arm and stepped around to the other side of Trent, squatting down so he could look more closely at his head, trying to see where the mysterious injury had occurred. He wanted to get a better look at what had happened to his son. We had been told that Trent had not died due to drowning but because something had hit the back of his head. Later we would see the autopsy report that blamed death on "multiple contusions to the head." Whatever hit him—maybe a boat, maybe a piece of coral—it had knocked him out and prevented him from surfacing for air.

Dad straightened up, and said, "OK, let's go."

I bent again to kiss Trent's forehead, then we walked out. We had been there less than ten minutes. It was the last time I would ever see my beautiful Trent.

I wish now that I could have stayed longer. I wish I could have had some time alone with Trent to talk with him, pray beside him, sing to him.

THE EXCRUCIATING PROCESS

Dad must have handled whatever paperwork was needed at the morgue. I was too numb to notice but walked, zombie-like, back to the car. Then Matthew drove us to our next stop: the police station. A Jamaican police officer took the report, and the interview became a long, agonizing ordeal. I struggled to understand his heavily accented English, and he laboriously wrote out my answers on his pad of paper:

"So . . . today is Sep-tem-ber e-lev-enth," he said to himself as he wrote on the pad. "And your name is?"

"Tammy Lenderink, T-a-m-m-y . . . L-e-n . . ."

"Sorry. Could you start again?"

"T-a-m . . ."

"And the last name?"

Emotionally and physically exhausted, I turned to Dad, my eyes begging him to help me. He slowly spelled out the letters of my name, Trent's name, and his name. It seemed to take forever. But we had just begun. Next the officer wanted a moment-by-moment account of everything we had done since we had arrived in Jamaica a week earlier. Like the morgue employees, he showed no feeling at all. He could just as well have been writing out a traffic ticket while I sat there constantly wiping away tears and trying to stay strong enough to speak.

After a couple of hours of this excruciatingly slow process, Matthew came in. He had been waiting in the car, and I couldn't believe what he said to the police officer: "Enough is enough!" he barked. "She has been through way too much already today. This is ridiculous. I'm taking her home. We are leaving. Do you have all you need, because we're going home."

The police officer looked up, surprised, just as Matthew turned to me and said, "Come on, Tammy." No one moved to stop us, so we walked back to the car, and Matthew drove us back to the Blue Lagoon. Rather than taking us back to the doctors' home, this time he took us to that beautiful house Trent and I had admired as we'd driven in that first day.

Was it just yesterday?

THE BEAUTIFUL HOUSE

"Trent, look at that house," I had said. "Isn't it amazing? Wouldn't it be cool to live in a place like that?" And he had answered, "Someday maybe we will, baby." Now Dad Lenderink and I were to stay there, in that beautiful home. It was Valerie's house, and she had graciously opened it to us. Now that Dad Lenderink was there, we needed two rooms, and the doctors only had one guest room.

It was a marvelous place. Valerie lived on one side of the home and sometimes rented out the other part of the house to tourists. Guests slept upstairs and came down to cross a little catwalk that passed over flowing water to get to the dining room. A cook and servants provided thoughtful and efficient service. It truly was an incredible place, and as I settled in, I kept thinking that Trent would have flipped out if he could have been there. The place was so cool—in more ways than one. Valerie's big, comfortable home had air conditioning! I was so thankful to her for taking us in.

I settled into the cozy room, my heart aching and my head spinning. So much had happened in such a short time. Just two nights before, I had fallen asleep beside Trent in a world that seemed steady and secure. Now, just forty-eight hours later, I felt as if I had lost everything. Trent was dead, and the whole world had erupted in chaos. I had only caught bits and pieces of the news throughout the day. Lost in my own grief, I could barely imagine that the same grief I was feeling was being shared that night by the families of nearly three thousand others.

Valerie tapped on the door then opened it a crack to stick her head inside. "Come on in," I told her. With tears in her eyes, she handed me Trent's watch. When his body was recovered and brought to the dock at her restaurant, she was afraid something would happen to it. So she had someone take it off Trent's wrist, and now she was delivering it to me. Even though she wasn't supposed to do it, she had known what would be important to me, and she had taken his watch to give to me. Seeing it now, I was reminded that Trent's wedding band was probably in his Dopp kit; he never wore it when he was diving for fear of losing it. So I hurried to find it and felt greatly relieved when I did.

Valerie smiled sweetly and backed out of the door, closing it as she left. I crawled in between the soft sheets, Trent's watch on my arm and his ring on my finger, with my own wedding band keeping it from falling off. And finally, I slept.

I would have preferred to sleep right on through the evening and into the night, but a few hours later another tap on the door awakened me. Dad Lenderink said softly, "Tammy, they've prepared some supper for us. I think it would be nice if you could come down and join us. Could you do that?"

I wanted to say, "No! I don't want to join anyone for dinner. I don't want to sit around a table and make chitchat with people I barely know. Can't I just stay here and be by myself and rest?"

But I didn't say that. Instead, I nodded OK and made my way down the stairs and into the dining area. I sat through dinner, half-hearing the others as they talked about the Blue Lagoon, about the beautiful house. I remember hearing Valerie ask, "What do you do, Tom?" Dad answered and then asked about Valerie's career. It all seemed like some kind of superficial stage play, and as I listened, the tears again began to roll. I stayed fifteen to twenty minutes, then I asked Valerie softly, "Would you excuse me please? I'm sorry, but would you excuse me?"

I went back to my room, curled up on the bed, and heard the phone ring somewhere in the house. A few seconds later there was a knock at my door. "Tammy, it's your mom on the phone," Valerie said. The calls continued throughout the evening—Aunt Donie, Gina, Pam, and my friends were letting me know I was in their hearts and in their prayers. I loved those calls; they were very healing for me, because I just wanted to be home so bad. I wanted this all to be over.

The next day, some people came from the American embassy, and they were very kind and caring. Surprisingly, many Jamaicans came too. Even though they didn't know me, they knew Valerie or they lived nearby and heard about my situation, and they simply came to express their condolences. Most of the time, they were believers, and they came, not knowing that I was one too. They came to offer words of comfort, and when we began talking, we discovered our mutual faith. It was an awesome gift.

Valerie and Matthew were kind and caring too, and Tom and I were grateful for a chance to witness to them. Matthew was a rough-and-tough guy, and Valerie said it was touching to see how devotedly he took care of me. She loved seeing this kindness come out of her son.

WAITING FOR TRENT

We couldn't have gone home even if we had wanted to go then, because no one was flying into the U.S. yet. But I was adamant that I wasn't leaving Jamaica without Trent. Meanwhile, paperwork and other requirements had to be completed before the Jamaican government would release the body to be shipped back to America.

Dad Lenderink handled everything, for which I was grateful.

Representatives from Food for the Poor came, shocked by what had happened and sadly coming to share my grief and my faith. They sent someone to drive my rental car back to the agency and turn it in, and they loaded Dad and me into a car and drove us to Kingston, more than three hours away. Dad held me in his arms as I softly cried all the way to the city. They took us to the hotel where Trent and I were to have stayed for the mission part of the trip. Now I was checking in with my father-in-law, and Trent was dead.

LOST IN GRIEF

Dad asked for adjoining rooms so he could keep an eye on me. I didn't leave my room for four days, didn't even take a shower for four days. Some of those days, I never even left my bed except to go to the bathroom and come back. I ate a little fruit and drank a little water; I lost ten pounds.

When I mustered some strength, I went through everything in the suitcases, crying as I caressed my cheek with Trent's clothes. I slept in his boxers and T-shirts; I was trying desperately to reach that smell, *Trent's* smell. Every night I would spray on his cologne so I would smell it through the night.

Throughout this time, Dad Lenderink was taking care of the arrangements, pleading with the Jamaican officials to release Trent's body, and trying to be ready with airline reservations as soon as they started flying again. Meanwhile, he was forging a stronger friendship with the people back at the Blue Lagoon who had been so helpful to us. So he was in and out of the hotel while I stayed there, curled up in a fetal position on the bed. Always wanting to do the right thing, he had encouraged me to continue my plans with Food for the Poor. "You know, Tammy, you've come this far . . . ," he said gently.

But I was absolutely unable to do it. I told him, "Dad, I'm in no shape to go on a mission trip, and I think they will understand that."

What I craved most of all during that time was my mom's loving embrace. Dad offered me comfort, but it wasn't the same as a mother's.

I admired Dad for handling all the papers and the arrangements and for finding productive ways to stay busy during the long, hard days when we were waiting for the airlines to start flying again—and for Trent's body to be released. While he managed to stay busy, I seemed to struggle for every movement, every breath. I had been so totally absorbed in my own grief that it really hadn't sunk in what had happened back in America. Then one afternoon I turned on the TV in my hotel room, and saw the people in New York holding up pictures of their loved ones with little notes that asked, "Have you seen my husband?" "Have you seen my mom?" All I could do was cry for them, remembering again how I had felt on the evening of September 10.

Watching those hurting people hold up their signs, I understood their grief, because on the night I lost Trent, I felt as if I were lifting up my own sign toward heaven and asking, "Can you find my husband, Jesus? Can you bring him back to me?" And, watching the sign-holders, I appreciated again the relief I'd felt when Trent's body was found. Even though the pain was excruciating, I was able to reach closure. I could say, "Thank you, Jesus, for bringing Trent back to me, even in death, because I don't know what I would have done if his body hadn't been found." I connected with those people in New York, and I wept for them. Even now, the tears come quickly when I think that some of them have nothing more of their loved one than a jar of dust scooped from Ground Zero.

The images were so painful that I didn't watch much TV as the days passed in my hotel room. But late one night when I couldn't sleep, I turned it on and was thankful to find a Christian station. And even better, there were my friends in the Christian musical group Selah. They were singing a song I recognized immediately, and at that moment I felt as if they were singing it solely to me. The song was "Press On," and I sat there singing along with them, "In Jesus's name, press on."

I crawled off the bed and knelt beside it, just like in those old pictures. I knelt there and put my hands up and prayed again and again, "In Jesus's name, press on." Over thousands of miles—and without even knowing it—my friends were ministering to me.

Another friend, Carman, reached out directly to me while we were stuck in Jamaica. He called one day to let me know he was praying for me. He had lost a brother, he said, so he knew what loss was. He'd been hurt that during that time no one in the industry had really reached out to him; now he wanted to reach out to me.

While we were talking, there was a knock on the door of my hotel room. I excused myself from the conversation with Carman and opened the door to find a camera aimed at me, and beside it were two reporters. One of them said, "Could we come in and just take a picture of you, do a story?"

I was shocked. "No! No, I can't—I don't want anybody to come in," I said. "I can't talk. I don't want a picture."

The reporter persisted. "Could we just come in and get a picture of you holding the pillow?"

"No, please. I can't. I'm sorry. I can't do that," I stuttered. And I closed the door.

I was crying when I came back to the phone. Carman said, "What's going on?"

I told him about the reporters, and he said, "Tammy, I'm going to hang up now, but I'll call you right back." So we hung up. And in a few moments he called back. He had called the hotel's security people and told them, "I do not want one more person going up to that room! Do you understand? You are not to give out that room number; I don't want anybody going up there!" Then he called me back and told me what he'd done.

"Thank you, Carman," I said gratefully. I wasn't bothered again by reporters.

After that, the hotel staff was more protective of me. One employee brought me free food each evening. I hardly ate anything, but she started bringing me grapes and other little bits of fruit to keep me going. Then one night she brought me a plaque that had the "Footprints in the Sand" story on it. Someone had given it to her during a rough time, she said, and she had taken it off her own wall to give to me.

Dad Lenderink and I spent quite a bit of time talking with each other, and while I know he meant well, just like any father would want to do—fix everything right then and take care of the situation—sometimes his words added to my heartache. I was thankful that he was stepping in and handling all the grueling details of getting us back to the

States, but when he extended that oversight into my future, I was rattled. He said, "Tammy, we need to set up a board of directors to manage you now that Trent's gone. We could have a board that helps you run your ministry, keep everything going, and helps you make decisions for your life."

Too numb most of the time to think about my next breath, let alone any time after that, I let most of what he was saying simply roll over me without registering. But I did let him know I didn't want a board of directors. And anyway, I might not even have a career, a ministry, when this whole nightmare was over.

Other times, Dad would reminisce about Trent. Obviously he was grieving just as I was. But I must admit that the hardest thing to hear at that time in my life was when he told me how lucky I was to have married Trent. Now, that statement I totally agreed with. But then he added, "You know, after all, Trent could have had anybody he wanted, but he chose you, and you know, Tammy, you were like damaged goods."

He was referring to the fact that I was the child of divorced parents, the product of a broken home. I knew Dad obviously wasn't thinking clearly, because he's not the kind of person who would deliberately cause someone pain, but his words struck a very painful blow to my already battered heart. I knew I hadn't been the perfect wife. I knew I could have been so much more to Trent. But being labeled "damaged goods" was hard to hear.

I went into the other room and cried as I thought back through our lives together. I was painfully reminded of the times I had hurt Trent when I had broken up with him while we were dating—or later, when I'd said or done something hurtful after we were married. Those memories brought feelings of guilt, regret, and shame. In that turmoil of emotions, I wondered if Trent really knew how much I loved him.

More than a year later, I admitted to Dad Lenderink how much his words had hurt me, and he immediately wrote back and apologized. He said, "You are absolutely right, and I am sorry I ever said those things. I never meant them intentionally, Tammy, and I apologize. Please forgive me. You know I love you."

Each day I was in Jamaica, I spoke with Mom, Gina, and Pam as well as other friends and family members. One day Mom asked if I would like her and Gina to drive to Nashville and get some things from our house. When we got to leave Jamaica with Trent's body, we would be going home to Michigan, not to Nashville. I had left home heading for a vacation trip; I didn't have the things I needed for a funeral. So I said yes, I would be grateful if she could make that trip.

Pam and Steve drove Mom and Gina from Grand Rapids back to Tennessee. When Pam's flight (and everyone else's) was canceled on September 11, Steve had immediately driven from Nashville to Buffalo to get her. He told Pam later he cried all the way. Next they drove to Grand Rapids, believing I would be home within a day or two. But of course that didn't happen. Now Pam and Steve offered to drive Mom and Gina to Nashville to bring back some things for me.

Pam wrote later that the four of them "sang and prayed and worshiped" as they made the drive. "We laughed and cried, telling story after story about Trent and his loving and mischievous ways." As they got closer to our Nashville neighborhood, however, the mood grew somber. Pam and Steve lived just a few doors down from Trent and me. "As we came into the subdivision, I felt like I was having a heart attack," Pam said. "I was hyperventilating. I knew I could not go to Tammy and Trent's house. I just couldn't do it. I asked Steve instead to take me home."

Fifteen minutes later, Steve called Pam from our house. "Honey, it's so beautiful here, so peaceful," he told her. "There's an incredible sense of peace; the presence of Jesus is so strong in this house you can almost breathe it. You can feel the angels here, filling the place with praises and glory. You have to come down, Pam. It's OK. You'll see."

Pam nervously walked through the door. "I felt like I had walked through a portal into heaven itself," she told me. "I felt like I was floating. Everything seemed light and glowing and in slow motion. Every cell in my body felt love and peace in that place, and I thought, *Maybe this is just a little taste of what Trent's feeling right now.*

Mom and Gina were experiencing the same thing. They called me when they got there, and I asked, "What is it like? What do you feel?"

"It's so peaceful, Tammy," Gina said, echoing Pam and Steve's responses. "It's so peaceful here."

How I longed at that moment to be back in my home with them—and with Trent!

Later Gina called and said, "OK, Tammy, I'm sitting in your closet. What do you need?" What a trooper she was, carrying out my directions in that very painful setting. But we shared a few giggles too, with her teasing me about being so organized. I knew exactly where the clothes were that I needed. I would say, "Over to the left, at the bottom, there's a brown sweater."

Gina would say, "OK, I got it."

Then I would say, "OK, past Trent's shirts on the left are my shirts. If you could grab the white one and the blue one, and the pants are up at the top . . ."

Mom and Gina stayed in my home for two or three days, and they called me each day. We would talk about what I wanted them to bring. I asked them to bring Trent's beloved mountain bike and his scuba gear to put by his casket at the funeral. I wanted to have his favorite things nearby. I urged them to gather pictures off the walls and to bring all the greeting cards they could find that Trent and I had given each other over the years. I asked them to load everything into Trent's big Suburban and drive it back to Michigan. I knew I wouldn't be needing the Suburban anymore; it was our "ministry truck" that we used to haul equipment and backdrops and everything else when we were out on the road. I had never liked to drive the Suburban; it was just too big. And obviously I wouldn't need it now, because I wouldn't be going back on the road—not for a long time. Maybe not forever.

ONE SPECIAL ANGEL

For me, the long days of waiting in the Jamaican hotel continued, and each seemed longer than the day before. One night there was a huge party outside the hotel right below my windows. It was really loud—

music and laughing and a DJ shouting into a microphone—and it went on late, late into the night. I called the front desk repeatedly, but they said there was nothing they could do because the party wasn't on hotel property. I even called the police—twice—but the raucous noise continued. The desk clerk offered to move me to another room, but I was too tired to do that. Finally I dragged my bedding into the bathroom—sheets, blanket, pillows, everything. I closed the door and shoved a towel under it, then I wadded up bits of tissue and plugged up my ears. And that's where I spent the rest of that night, on the floor in the bathroom.

The next morning, I realized Dad Lenderink had left. (He had told me the night before that he was going back to the Blue Lagoon the next morning.) To be honest, I was kind of happy to have the day to myself, because I wanted to be able to cry and cry and cry and not have him feel as though he needed to come in and try to rescue me. I just wanted to cry. My heart was broken. My Trent was gone. I wanted my mom. And she couldn't get to me.

We kept thinking that I would be coming home soon. *Surely, the airlines will start flying again soon, and how long can this paperwork take?* So I was telling my family, "You guys stay home. With everything that's happened in America, do not try to fly down here. Who knows what's going to happen next? You're safe there, so you stay, and I'll be home soon. I need you guys. I can't understand this. But stay there. I'll be home soon."

That's what I told my mom and my sister and the friends who had tried to fly to Jamaica. But secretly I longed to have them with me. That morning, when I realized Dad was gone, I lay on the bathroom floor and wailed. I sobbed and moaned and cried so loudly the hard-tiled walls of the bathroom seemed to echo every sound.

In the midst of my brokenhearted tirade, I had this tearful conversation with God: "If all this is real, if you are real, if heaven is real," I sobbed, "could you just send somebody to hold me? God, could you just send somebody? I'm not asking for a hundred angels; I'm just asking for one special angel, just one angel who could hold me right now. God, you're so big . . . if you can hear me, if you care . . . please, do this for me."

Then I heard within me the words, *Get up and move.* Surprised and a little shaky, I got to my feet. It took every ounce of strength I possessed to move toward the door, open it, and step out into the room. I was bracing myself against the counter, leaning against the wall, trying to move. Weakly but determinedly dragging my bedclothes out of that bathroom, I thought later I must have looked like a female Lazarus, emerging from the tomb.

The tears were flowing again, and I held onto the door frame and peered out from the bathroom and through the adjoining doorway. A short, slightly chubby Jamaican woman wearing a Hilton housekeeping uniform was standing there in Dad's room. Suddenly I needed some order in my life; at that moment, I wanted things to be made right.

I wiped my face and said to her, "Excuse me, ma'am, but could you just come in and make my bed? I've got my sheets all wadded up in the bathroom, and I've made a mess of everything. Could you please come and make my bed?"

When she saw me, her beautiful, smooth, black face reshaped itself into a sympathetic expression of concern. "Oh! I've been trying to get to you," she exclaimed with her sweet Jamaican accent. "I could hear you crying, and I've been trying to get to you."

Then she paused and took a step toward me. "Could I just come and hold you?" she asked.

The moment she stepped toward me, I started to cry again, nodding my head, biting my lip, tears coursing down my cheeks. She had heard me as I'd lain on the floor of that bathroom and cried out to God.

Who knew angels wore Hilton housekeeping outfits? She was an instant answer to prayer, a godsend. She wrapped her arms around me, and I dropped my head onto her shoulder and sobbed. I felt so comforted in that moment, so reassured that God is real. All my life I had taken Jesus for granted, just always assumed he was there, an invisible but ever-present force in my life. That morning I had asked him for an angel . . . and here she was. As she held me, I felt the arms of Jesus embracing me, comforting me, supporting me.

With my head against her shoulder, she started whispering into my ear. At first I couldn't understand, but then it became clear. *Of course! She's praying for me, exactly what an angel would do.*

Then she held me back to look into my face. "You're grieving, aren't you?" she asked with concern covering her face. "You've lost someone, haven't you?"

"Yes," I whispered. "My husband."

"Oh, no! But you're so young!" She prayed again, eyes closed, earnest words winging themselves upward.

She hugged me again. And when I felt strong enough to stand on my own, she eased away from me and said, "Now, just let me straighten your room for you; I'll make your bed for you."

I moved into Dad's room and waited for her to finish. She flung a clean sheet up into the air and let it settle back onto the bed. As she worked, she sang. It took me a moment to realize what I was hearing. She was totally off-key, but the words were clear. She was singing praises to the Lord, and it was the most beautiful sound I've ever heard. It was as if my tone-deaf Trent were singing to me, and to Jesus, through this gentle angel in the housekeeping outfit.

I smiled, listening to her as I sat at the desk in Dad's room. The Gideon Bible was lying there, and I reached for it. *Speak to me through your Word, God. Please, don't make me hunt for it. I'm too wrung out now to think clearly. Just let me open up this Bible and find a message to me from you. Please, Lord, don't make me climb a mountain, walk through a valley, and struggle through the jungle to figure out what you want me to know right now. I just ask you to meet me here and show me.*

I opened that Bible, and immediately my eye fell on a specific verse: Psalm 30:5. This is how I read that passage, *Although you may mourn throughout the night and sorrow will endure throughout the night—probably throughout many nights, Tammy—my joy will always come in the morning. My joy will always meet you in the morning. When you feel like you can't breathe, when you feel like you can't walk, when you can't see, when you can't get through the day, I'm still there, carrying you. When you can't breathe one more time, then just rest your head on the pillow, and I'll be right there beside you. When you wake up the next morning, I'll be right there beside you. My joy will cover you. And joy will be the very thing that will bring you back to life again, because without it, you'll never survive this grief. Just trust me, Tammy. Trust me.*

Amazed, even shocked by how vividly Jesus was reaching out to me, I rose from the desk and walked to the huge window, looking out over the city and the water. I stood there, staring out that window, and incredibly, I felt joy, unspeakable joy, heavenly joy. There was nothing in my life that made me happy at that moment, yet I felt unspeakable joy. Now I had one more request for Jesus: *Lord, if you could just show Trent a glimpse into my life right now, please let him see this. Let him know I'm going to be OK. Let him understand that he didn't do this to me and that you didn't do this to me. And Jesus, even though I don't understand any of this, I know somehow together you and I will survive.*

It was important for me to say that, to acknowledge both my confusion and my determination to cling to the truth: *I don't understand anything right now, Jesus, but I know you didn't do this to me. You love me more than that. You would never take Trent from me. I don't get it; I don't see how this could be good for my life. How could living without Trent be good for me? He was the only man who never left me. Now he's gone, and I don't understand. All I know is I trust you. You've been with me before. I've always been a fighter, always survived whatever came my way. So I guess I just have to fight through this thing too. I hate that I have to do that. But you've been with me before, and you'll be with me through this too.*

Standing there, marveling at what had happened to me, I began to understand why my mom and Gina and Pam had been unable to get to me. Trent had always been there whenever I needed help. He had been my savior, my comforter, my healer—all those things. When Trent was in my life, I would sometimes ask God for insight, some bit of guidance, and when it didn't come soon enough, I would go to Trent instead, asking, "Baby, what should I do? Trent was always there, and he always helped me figure out the answer.

Now I realized that if my mom had made it, if my sister or my dad or Pam had been able to get to me, they would have become my comforters. They would have saved me. Instead, I now felt Jesus telling me, *I'm all you've got, Tammy. I'm your healer, your comforter, your Savior, and when you go home, and six months from now, everybody's moved on and you're still stuck in this sorrow, working through this grief, I'm going to be right there with you. I'm the only One who's going to be there every single day for you.*

He was telling me, *Start listening for my voice, Tammy. Sometimes you struggle, wondering who's talking: Is it God? Or is it me? You don't always know, because you don't know what my voice is and what your voice is. Get into my Word, Tammy, and I'll talk to you. I'll guide you. We'll walk through this together.*

BLESSED BY BEING ABLE TO GIVE

After the maid had made my bed and cleaned my room, she peeked through the door into Dad's room and said to me, "I'll come back and bring you some more bottled water."

"Thank you," I said, trying to smile. As she turned toward the door into the hallway, I asked God, *What can I do for this woman, Jesus? She's given me so much. Now what can I give to her?*

I watched her walk away from me and looked her up and down. *What does she need, Jesus?* She was in that housekeeping outfit, so she looked just like every housekeeping staff member in the hotel. But then I noticed her shoes—or what was left of them. They were little more than scraps of leather—or maybe not even leather; they could have been pieces of vinyl, and they were held together with yarn, of all things—both of them.

It was quite awhile before I saw her again. She didn't come back right away, and I ended up going down to the pool with my Bible, feeling the sunshine on my face for the first time in days. I was back in my room awhile later when I heard her moving around again in Dad's room. I peeked through the door and waved at her. "I brought you your water, Miss Tammy," she said with a gentle smile on her beautiful face.

I said, "Hang on. I have something for you." I went back into my room and dug through the suitcase to find Trent's wallet. It held a wad of brand-new twenty-dollar bills. I pulled them all out and counted. There was nearly two hundred dollars there. I started to put the wallet away then realized I'd better save a few bills for myself; I put some of the money back in the wallet.

Returning to Dad's room, I handed her the money. "You've been such a gift to me," I told her. "God wants you to know that whatever you need, he's going to take care of you, just like he's taking care of me. He loves you wherever you are. So this isn't from me; it's from God, to remind you that he loves you so much."

As I handed her the bills, she started to cry. "Oh, Miss Tammy!" she said. "You have no idea what this means to me. This is an answer to prayer—oh, Jesus! Jesus!" She told me, "I didn't even know how I was going to get to work today. My car broke down two weeks ago; it's been at the shop all this time, and it's still there because I don't have the money to fix it. So I had to take a taxi—had to spend a *dollar* to take a taxi to come here. I'm a single mom, and my children and I, we have nothing. Oh, Miss Tammy, you have no idea. Thank you, Jesus!"

I said, "Hang on. There's something more he wants you to have." I went back in that room, and I was giddy, thinking that the money in Trent's wallet had been hers all along. It just took me awhile to figure out God wanted me to give it to her! I handed her the rest of the money and said, "This is all yours. This is supposed to be for you." Then we both started giggling; she was crying as she brushed away the tears, and I was laughing—what a strange feeling, to laugh again. I was so excited to realize I'd heard from God. I had asked, *What does she need?* And he had shown me the answer.

In the worst time of my life, in the greatest loss I've ever known, being able to *give* to somebody was wonderful. I was thankful to be in a place where God allowed me to give. It was a huge turning point for me; from that moment on, I knew that, no matter how difficult things got in the days ahead, I would, once again, survive. I would be OK. Even today, I cherish the memory of the joy I received that day when I found a way to *give* in the midst of enormous loss.

16

ONE SUMMER DAY, Trent's nephew Trey spotted a little water snake in the lake and wanted to see it up close. He asked Uncle Trent if he would catch it for him. Trent went into the water and caught the snake, and in the process he was bitten. Trey felt bad, seeing the blood, as Trent was showing him the snake.

"Trey, you are certainly worth bleeding for," Trent told him. "Just think of the blood Jesus shed for me." . . .

Trent's death has been our personal Ground Zero, but God does not want us to stay at Ground Zero. We praise God and lift his name and thank him for the blessing of Trent's life in our lives.

—A reminiscence from Sally Anne Lenderink,
Trent's mother

16 | remembering trent

HE AIRLINES WERE FLYING AGAIN, and finally, after eleven days, the Jamaican authorities released Trent's body so we could take him home. I sat on the plane, staring out that window, as tears raced down my face. I was trying to get a glimpse of the casket, wanting to know that Trent was there. I had an urgent feeling that if he wasn't on the plane I couldn't live with it. I couldn't bear the thought of landing in Chicago and finding out there had been a glitch and his casket hadn't made it onto the plane. I had come so far, I didn't want to leave without him at the very end. So I was watching everything that was happening around the plane, but I couldn't see anything that looked like a casket.

Feeling the same way I did, Dad Lenderink got up and asked the gate agent to check and make sure everything was OK. He assured us it was.

What an awful, gut-wrenching thing to sit on that plane, peering out the window, watching Jamaica disappear from view, and thinking about how things should have been. I wished with all my heart that Trent was sitting there beside me, holding my hand as he always did, whispering his little take-off prayer again: "Thank you, Jesus, for this day. Protect us, Lord, as we fly. In Jesus' name, amen."

Instead, I was sitting by my father-in-law, and Trent was below, in the cargo hold, in a casket. And my life would never be the same. I thought, *Here I am, breathing, on a plane, and Trent's on this plane but he's not breathing.*

QUIET HOMECOMING

We flew nonstop to Chicago, arriving close to midnight. Dad had decided it would be better to do things that way, because in Grand Rapids, our hometown, reports of Trent's death were all over the news, all over Christian radio, and he thought there might be reporters or a crowd of people waiting at the airport if news leaked out that we were flying into Grand Rapids. Instead, Dad wisely arranged for us to fly into Chicago.

A Grand Rapids funeral home was there to take the casket home from the airport, and Trent's brother Troy was there to meet us. We walked out of the baggage claim area at O'Hare after going through customs, and there he stood next to a rented Lincoln, the backdoor open and waiting for me. He held out his arms for a hug then helped me into the car.

Troy had been with Dad in Los Angeles when the call came that Trent was missing. While Dad had flown immediately to Jamaica, Troy had driven straight through from the West Coast back to Grand Rapids to be with the rest of the family. Now he had brought the comfortable car to take us home. Mom Lenderink had sent along a pillow and blanket; a rose lay on the pillow, and she had sent along some potpourri and some lotion too, as well as a little cooler filled with snacks and bottled water. Next to the pillow was a bag full of cards addressed to me from family, friends, and fans. What a thoughtful person Mom Lenderink was to have made those provisions for me, and how smart Dad had been to arrange things this way.

There were no cameras flashing in my face, and not even a big mob of family ready to fall on me. Troy played a CD of soothing praise music all the way home and occasionally asked if I needed anything. He and Dad talked softly in the front seat, and I felt lots of love as I understood the planning that had gone into this poignant trip.

Finally, in the wee hours of the morning, we pulled up in front of Mom and Keith's house, and I fell into Mom's arms for the embrace I had been craving for nearly two weeks. Gina and Ken were there too, and we hugged and cried together until we were finally cried out.

Mom had everything set for me in the downstairs bedroom where Trent and I always slept when we visited. She had our pictures out and some candles glowing. Exhausted, I crawled into bed, and she sat beside me, rubbing my feet and my back for an hour or so until I fell asleep.

The next morning we all went to the funeral home, nearly a dozen of us—Mom and Dad Lenderink as well as Troy and Tracey, one of Trent's sisters. My mom and my brother were there, too, along with Gina and her husband, Ken. The service had to be planned, and decisions had to be made. But I was too numb to decide much of anything, so most of the time I sat silently, listening while the others spoke up, providing names and details for the obituary and offering suggestions for the service. I did say I didn't want to have visitation. I had been walking out this tragedy for the last two weeks, and I didn't have the strength to go through two days of visitation. "I just can't draw this out anymore," I said.

I also decided that the service would be closed-casket. I knew that Trent wouldn't want anybody to see him not looking his best. But at the same time, those who were closest to Trent—some members of his family and mine—wanted that closure. So I told them that I was leaving it up to them. "If you really want to see Trent, you can; I'm not going to make that decision for you. If you can handle it, then do what you think is best for you, but I don't want to replace the image I have of Trent with anything less than that. And as far as other people and strangers seeing him in the casket, I know Trent wouldn't like that."

Then the funeral director spoke up, "I really would not advise it," he said seriously. "I would not advise it at all. It's been a long time, and he doesn't look good. He doesn't look like you remember him. So I wouldn't advise it."

They decided to heed his advice, but I think some of them may regret the decision now, feeling as though they're still looking for closure. I wanted to remember Trent as he'd been that last day before he swam into the Blue Lagoon—so handsome that I had stopped him to take his picture as he pulled on his wet suit. That was the same Trent I had seen the next day in the morgue. I thank God for giving me that last perfect glimpse of him.

We set up the details of the memorial service, then it was time to go downstairs to pick out the casket. I walked into that room with the rest of the family beside me and saw all of those caskets on display, and the grief washed over me again. I fell to the floor, sobbing my heart out. "This isn't happening!" I moaned. My mom and Mom Lenderink were on their knees beside me, rubbing my back and crying along with me. The others started praying aloud, and I simply lay there on the floor, letting their prayers flow over me until I was able to pull myself together. Finally back on my feet, I trembled as I tried to catch my breath, then I started walking around, doing what had to be done. We picked out a casket made of some kind of beautiful wood. Since wood had been such a part of Trent's family's life, we all knew that was the right choice.

A TRIBUTE TO TRENT

The service was at First Assembly of God in Grand Rapids, the same church where Trent and I had met nearly eighteen years earlier. I'll never forget walking down that long aisle of the church, staring straight ahead at the casket. I couldn't help but remember walking down another aisle in that same church eleven years earlier, wearing my wedding dress, my heart galloping with joy as I looked down front to see my gorgeous husband-to-be beaming back at me. It was a big church, so it was a long aisle. My mom and my dad walked beside me now, holding me, supporting me, as we made our way to the front where Trent now lay in his casket.

Behind us were Dad's wife, Val, and Mom's husband, Keith, walking arm in arm, and then the rest of Trent's family and mine.

A few nights before the funeral, Mom and Keith had invited Dad and Val, along with some other friends, to their house for dinner, and once again I had been thankful that Trent had helped restore my family. And just like a little girl, I crawled onto Dad's lap out on the porch that night while Mom, Keith, and Val chatted in the kitchen as Mom put the finishing touches on dinner. Hearing their voices trickle through the screen door, I thought, *This is unbelievable. It's a treasured legacy from Trent. I can't imagine not having them all here, all together now, when I need them most.*

I was even more grateful at the funeral to have Mom and Dad walking together with me, standing together with me, all the old bitterness replaced by friendship and respect.

To all you divorced parents out there, I ask that you learn from my story what it means to a child to have parents who, although they no longer love each other, come together to love their children unconditionally and keep any bitterness to themselves. Try with all your might to be friends so that your children can know the blessing of having two parents willing to come together when undivided support is needed most of all. You never know when those situations may arise.

My parents were together for me at Trent's funeral, for which I will be forever grateful. My mom sang a beautiful song, then it was my turn to speak. I had written out most of what I wanted to say and hoped I would be able to get through it. I stood up as Mom was waiting on the platform for me so she could offer me support after her song, but as I started to take that first step, my knees buckled, and I staggered, as though I just didn't have the strength to move. Once again, I couldn't breathe, couldn't catch my breath. I felt like I was the one who was drowning now. Immediately Dad sprang up and caught me. My mom reached for me as well, and they led me up to the pulpit and stood beside me, holding on to me, as I read my tribute to Trent, standing there, looking down on his casket.

I reminded everyone what an incredible man Trent had been in my life—and in most of their lives as well. "He always spoke life to me," I said. "Trent always covered me with his love." I ended the eulogy by saying, "I know I will see Trent again because I believe in Christ, because I believe in heaven, because I believe in salvation. But until then . . . 'The LORD is my shepherd; I shall not want. He maketh me to lie down in green pastures; he leadeth me beside the still waters. He restoreth my soul; he leadeth me in the paths of righteousness for his name's sake. Yea, though I walk through the valley of the shadow of death, I will fear no evil,' for Jesus is right here beside me. . . ."

Mingled with the tears that day, there was also laughter. A video was shown of Trent and his high school friend Gordie appearing in the play *Heaven's Gates, Hell's Flames,* which was performed each year for several years at First Assembly. Gordie and Trent, who loved being involved in acting and drama, were cast as construction workers.

In their scene, they're taking a break from their construction job, eating lunch. One of them (Gordie) is saved; the other one (Trent) isn't. Gordie tells Trent about Jesus and all the stuff of the gospel, and Trent is incredulous. "You can live forever? Really? *Really?*" It's a funny part of the play, and Trent and Gordie were hilarious. Each year when the play was presented, the audience would laugh hysterically as the two guys hammed it up.

That was the video that was shown at Trent's memorial service. Pam Thum's parents had written the play (but later gave up their rights to it); one of them had remembered that Trent's performance had been videotaped, and it became an extraordinary part of his memorial service.

As the scene continues, Trent accepts the Lord. And right after he does so, a beam falls on them, killing them both. Then we flash into the next scene, and Trent and Gordie are in heaven, standing in front of an angel who is checking the Book of Life, looking for their names. Gordie asks, "Is my name there? Is my name in the Book of Life?" The angel looks, and yes, there it is.

Then Trent steps up. "Hey, angel. How ya doin'? I *know* my name is there. Go ahead. Look," he says, winking at her.

The angel looks. She doesn't see it. "I *know* it's gotta be there," Trent says. "Keep looking." He carefully spells out his stage name as the angel turns the pages and runs her finger up and down the columns of names. Finally she finds it, and she opens the gates of heaven for him. Trent is deliriously happy, jumping for joy, bouncing around the stage like someone on a pogo stick. "Thank you, angel! Thank you!" He skips merrily through the gates and runs up the stairs into heaven.

It is an amazing scene. Absolutely stunning. The impact it had that day was obvious. At the end of the service, sixty people came forward to give their lives to Jesus. They too wanted to know that their name is written in the Book of Life. Like Trent, they wanted to someday go bounding through the gates of heaven.

Burial was to be another day. At the end of the memorial service, the family was to leave first, then we were to get into cars and make the thirty-minute drive to the Lenderinks' home. They had erected a huge tent and planned to host a reception there.

The plans changed as I led the family back down the aisle. As I stepped into the church lobby, there were already a few friends standing there, waiting to greet me. So I stepped toward them and hugged one of them, then another, and another, and within a few minutes there was a line of hundreds of people waiting to hug me.

The Lenderinks left, heading home to host the reception, but I decided to stay. I knew I needed to hug those friends as much as they needed to hug me. They needed to know that I would be OK. Some of them had come a long way to remind me they loved me, and staying there to acknowledge that love seemed like the least I could do.

My precious sister Gina stood right beside me, whispering to the next person in line, "Please don't cry, and please keep it short." She was great at protecting me and keeping the line moving. So instead of being the first one to leave the church that day . . . I was the last.

By the time I got to the Lenderinks' home, the reception was in full swing. There was every kind of food imaginable, and people were waiting there to speak to me. But by then I was emotionally and physically at the end of my rope, and although I ventured into the tent for a few minutes, I quickly retreated to the room Mom Lenderink had prepared for me. Mom and Gina and a few other family members stayed with me there. Occasionally someone would peek in the door and say, "There are a lot of people out there waiting to see you, Tammy." I did go out a couple of times, but I didn't stay long; I simply couldn't take any more.

NERDS AND A DOVE

We all agreed Trent's burial would be a private affair, with just family and close friends attending. Trent would be buried in a beautiful spot on the Lenderinks' land. Troy had mentioned the idea while Dad and I were still in Jamaica, and I had agreed that Trent would have loved it. Troy worked hard to get all the right permissions and permits so that the plot is designated as an official family cemetery. We buried Trent there a few days after the memorial service.

Our pastor at First Assembly told me we didn't really need a pastor there to officiate because we had already completed the committal service and the blessing at the funeral. So I asked Mom Lenderink if we could all just go out there together and have a beautiful day among ourselves, and she agreed. We would share our thoughts and memories about Trent, read some favorite Scripture verses, sing a song, or do whatever we wanted.

And that's what we did.

We gathered in that beautiful clearing in the forest. We surrounded the casket, Dad Lenderink began with prayer, then I said a few things about Trent and sang a song that had meant a lot to both of us. Next Gina shared a wonderful memory about him, and my brother, Norm, blew a ram's-horn shofar. Norm's a trumpet player, and the sound he got out of that thing was amazing.

Then Norm's father-in-law (his wife, Diana's, father, John DeVries) brought me a single white dove, gently passing it from his hands to mine. The DeVries family has trained a flock of doves that they rent out for weddings and similar events. The doves circle the site where they're released then fly away home.

Diana had wanted to be the one to hand the dove to me, but she was nervous about accidentally letting it go and ruining the moment. There was no way I was letting that little thing go, although the dove *was* antsy as I cupped its trembling body in my hands while my mom read a beautiful little essay about its symbolism. The dove pecked at some sparkling rhinestones on my red shirt and every second or two turned to look at me as if to ask, *Now?*

Finally I lifted my hands and released the dove, imagining it was Trent I was releasing from his earthly life to fly away to heaven. The little bird fluttered upward then circled the clearing twice before flying away. It was such a sweet, poignant moment. And you know what? Diana's family told us later that every dove they've ever released in the last seven years has always come home to them. But not this dove! That dove took off, and it has never come back. I smile every time I think of it off adventuring out there somewhere. That is so Trent!

Kenny and Kyle had a special thing to share. A couple of weeks before we left for Jamaica, Trent and I were visiting with Gina and her family. The boys had just watched a movie about a football player who had died; at his funeral, someone had placed a football in the casket. Kenny asked, "Why did they do that? Why did they put a football in his casket?"

Gina and Ken have always tried to be as open as possible with their boys, even about the difficult things in life. Knowing that, Trent sat at the table with Kenny and Kyle and explained why family and friends might want to put something special in a loved one's casket. He told the boys, "Now, when Uncle Trent dies, you can be sad for a little while, but then you have to be happy because Uncle Trent will be with Jesus. OK, now let's think of something you could put in my casket. How about candy? I love candy! And one of my favorites is Nerds. You may have to search the Internet to find them then, because that's gonna be a long time from now, and they may not be around then. But you can probably find them offered on the Internet."

That had been Trent's last conversation with his godsons. So naturally the boys had insisted that there had to be Nerds at the burial, and indeed there were. Trent's close friend Scott had a basket full of them, and he passed it around for everyone to share. Then, instead of laying the traditional flower on the casket, we all sprinkled Nerds everywhere. We imagined Trent getting a big kick out of that, and of course it was something special and even fun for Kenny and Kyle in that somber place.

As difficult as it was for us to accept his death, Trent seemed to have reached out from the grave to help us find a way to smile again.

17

Tammy,
 I just wanted to say thank you for choosing to sing songs that inspire people like me, who have reached the very end of their path and are stumbling in darkness.

—a note from a fan

17 | going home

I NEEDED TO SELL THE HUGE SUBURBAN, but in those weeks immediately following 9/11, nobody was buying cars, so the dealerships were struggling. The Suburban's *Blue Book* value was fourteen thousand dollars. So I called Todd Schuiteman, whose family owns a car dealership in Fremont, Michigan. Todd is like a son-in-law to the Lenderinks because his wife, Cheryl, was one of their "adoptees" more than twenty years ago and is still considered part of the family today. But Todd could only offer me eight thousand dollars.

"Trent would shoot me if I let you have it for that," I told Todd.

So I put a sign on it and parked it in front of Mom's house. Two days later, a man stopped by and said, "I love that truck." He wanted to drive it. So I climbed in with him, and we took it for a drive. He asked why I was selling it and was shocked when I told him. Two days later he bought it for fourteen thousand dollars. Tearfully, I watched out the front window of Mom's house as he drove it away.

Later I told Todd I had gotten full price for the Suburban, and he said, "Girl, you've gotta come work for us, because we're not selling anything right now!"

I stayed at Mom's house a little more than a month. My dear Nashville neighbor, Karyn Meucci, went to the post office every Monday to collect my mail and send it to me via FedEx. Still, things were piling up, and I knew it was time to go home. I had stayed away as long as I could, and now I knew I had to try to start my life over again without Trent.

Mom and Gina flew back with me, and it was a difficult day. We didn't say a lot to each other; a blanket of dread seemed to surround us. But there was a strong feeling of love binding us, and we were all trying to be strong for each other.

For some reason I felt it was important to come into my house by myself the first time, even without Mom and Gina. The only way to do that and not leave them waiting out on the driveway was for us to be picked up separately. So I asked another neighbor, Shannon Litten, to pick me up, and Pam and Steve would pick up Mom and Gina and bring them a little later. I probably caused unnecessary complications in setting it up this way, but no one argued with me. They knew this would be a stressful time for me, and everyone was willing to be a little inconvenienced to help me.

Shannon and her husband, Dirk, had been good neighbors to Trent and me; we had enjoyed some happy times together, and I wanted to have just a little time with Shannon alone, hoping to minister to her and help her see that while I was heartbroken to have lost Trent, I was completely sure I would see him again in heaven. We didn't say a lot on the ride from the airport. But when we pulled into our neighborhood, I began crying. Shannon reached over and took my hand, but neither of us said anything. She pulled into the driveway. "Are you sure you don't want me to go in with you, Tammy?" she asked.

"I'm sure. But thank you, Shannon," I told her.

"If you need anything, you know I'm here." She lived just a couple of doors away.

I nodded, thanked her, and gave her a hug.

Then I punched in the code to open the garage door. Hearing the familiar noise as it rumbled up, out of the way, a morsel of memory flashed through my mind: Trent and me coming out through the garage, carrying our luggage to Pam and Steve's car, big smiles on our faces, glad to see our friends and happy to be on our way to Jamaica.

My eyes fell on Trent's yard shoes, lined up next to the door leading into the house. He wore them when he was mowing the grass or working outside, and he always took them off before he came inside. I looked at those shoes and pictured Trent leaving them there, lifting out one foot, then the other.

I opened the door and stepped into the house. Everything was exactly as we had left it. There was the DVD lying out beside the TV: *Patch Adams*. We had watched it together the night before we left for Jamaica. Trent loved that movie, and we had both wiped away tears at the end, where Patch loses the love of his life.

I walked quietly through the house. I didn't weep uncontrollably, didn't moan or wail, but the tears rolled down my cheeks, and occasionally I covered my mouth to keep from sobbing aloud. I sat down in the living room and looked around, then I got up and walked through every room on the first floor.

Finally I started up the sixteen stairs, clinging to the stair rail to pull myself up every step. I stepped into our bedroom and looked around at everything as though I'd never seen it before. And yet it was all so familiar: the pillows arranged just so on the bed, the picture on the dresser, Trent's underwear on the floor. I smiled, remembering how I'd said, "Honey, pick that up," but in the rush to leave that morning, he'd obviously forgotten it.

In our bathroom, I rubbed my hand along the big bathtub we'd shared so many times. I imagined Trent sliding under the surface, holding his breath. There were candles all around the edge of the tub, and I noticed a little matchbook leaning against one of them. Not knowing why, I opened it up, and there, in Trent's writing, was a message to me: "Hi, TT!" He'd drawn a big heart around the words.

It was as if he had left that little matchbook for me to find at exactly that difficult moment. My heart lurched, imagining him writing the words.

Inside our walk-in closet, I pulled a bunch of Trent's clothes off the hangers and sank to the floor, burying my face in them. I lay there a long time—maybe forty-five minutes—weeping and trying to breathe in

Trent's scent, trying to feel his presence again in those rumpled clothes.

Finally I got up and walked out to the balcony overlooking the living room, and there were my precious mom and sister sitting quietly on the couch, waiting for me. They looked up at me and smiled, and I came down the stairs to curl up in their arms.

A PLACE OF PEACE

Mom said, "Remember what we told you, Tammy, when we came down here while you were still in Jamaica? It's so peaceful here. It's hard to believe, but it's so peaceful. Can you feel it too?"

I nodded. Despite all the hardships, all the difficulties, it felt good to be home.

When they had come to my house while I was still in Jamaica, Steve had booted up the computer in the office, looking for something I'd asked him to find. When he called with the information, he told me, "Tammy, there's something else on the computer . . ."

"What is it?" I'd asked.

"It's just something . . . well, just be sure to turn on the computer when you get home," he said. "It's something really neat."

Now, remembering what Steve had said, I eased off the couch and walked into the office. I pushed the button to start the computer and waited for the screen to light up. And then, there it was. I caught my breath when I saw it: a little yellow square in the lower left-hand corner. It looked like a sticky note stuck there on the screen, and it said, "Tammy is who I dream of. Can't wait to see you."

Can't wait to see you.

I sat there, stunned, by the messages Trent had left for me to find. First the matchbook, and now the computer. I was amazed how Trent continued to comfort me, even from heaven.

Gina stayed several days with me, and Mom stayed two weeks. Then, for almost a year, Mom came once a month or so, and Gina flew down from Chicago to be with me almost every weekend. Then she came every other weekend for another six months or so. What a gift they both were to me, and what a sacrifice they made to be with me—especially Gina and her boys and Ken. He has a stressful job, but what a thoughtful, self-less man he was to say so many times, "Go. We'll figure out how to take care of the boys. You need to be with your sister."

He was exactly right; Gina is one of my closest friends, and Ken was one of Trent's best friends. We had often traveled together on vacations—Ken, Gina, and the boys. Trent and Ken loved to go diving together.

Just a few months earlier we had spent a week together in Orlando; it was a trip we later called "the big surprise" because Kenny and Kyle hadn't known about it until the last minute. And they hadn't known Trent and I would meet them there. The four of them flew into the airport in Orlando and got a rental car. Then, as they were leaving the airport, Ken told the boys he had found a guy who needed a ride. Ken pulled up alongside a fat man who had his arm in a sling; he was wearing thick glasses and had a band-aid on his nose. Long strands of stringy hair fell out from under his hat, and he spoke with a deep southern drawl. The man got into the car, and the boys didn't know what to think; they were trying to be as polite as they could be, but they were bothered because the man kept commenting on how cute their mother was. Then the man gave a great big sneeze and pulled off his disguise. It was Trent—with a pillow stuffed under his shirt!

Everyone roared with laughter. It was a typical Trent moment—and only the beginning of a week full of fun. Ken and Trent spent a lot of time in the hotel's pool teaching the boys how to swim. Then the two men practiced hanging off the side of the pool, upside down in the water, holding their breath. Ken's best time was three and a half minutes; Trent's was more than five.

Trent had called Ken several times during July and August, trying to persuade him to bring Gina and come with us to Jamaica so they could dive together. But it was a busy time at Ken's job, and he couldn't get away. He has told me how difficult that decision has been for him since the accident. "I wish I'd gone," he told me. "If I had been there, maybe I could have made a difference. I would have been in the water with Trent; maybe, when whatever it was hit him on the head, I could have gotten to him in time to bring him up."

We'll never know, this side of heaven, why that wasn't part of God's plan. As Ken says, one thing we've learned from all this is that we don't always have the answers; instead we have to put our trust in God and find peace within his sovereignty.

CARRYING THE TORCH FOR TRENT

Gradually, I eased into life on my own. I agreed to do an interview with *The 700 Club* within a month of my return from Jamaica because I knew the staff members and trusted them to handle the interview with sensitivity. But after that, I declined other invitations to be interviewed or to perform. I had decided to take a year off after feeling God telling me, *Walk away from this stuff, Tammy. Come down off the platform and let me put your life back together again. I'm going to show you that my plan hasn't changed. Your plan changed, Tammy, and that's pretty hard for you. But my plan hasn't changed.*

During that year I thought a lot about destiny and our part in God's plan. It took me a long time to get to the point of believing maybe Trent's destiny was fulfilled. He so often questioned his purpose in life and wished to be used by God for something meaningful. Now I see more clearly the truth of what someone told me: Even when you think God's not using you, if you're walking in his will, *he's using you!* I see the godly influence Trent had on the people around him—his little godsons, his nieces and nephews, his brothers, sisters, and friends, and the hundreds of people he came in contact with through business dealings and in my music career. I could see them reacting to him the same way I did when we first met: *Here's a deeply spiritual man who is* fun *to be with.* Just as I did, they enjoyed being with Trent, and they wanted to have what he had—a deep, abiding joy that came from his faith in the Father and bubbled over into everything he did.

And personally, I see now that one of Trent's purposes was to be a man who would change the heart of a woman. Because that's certainly what he did for me; he changed my heart and prepared me for something greater. My goal now is to pass along the message of Trent's life and help others make changes in their lives that will lead them closer to God. And as I do so through my music and my witness, that part of God's plan for Trent surely is fulfilled.

These thoughts help ease the pain of losing Trent, but they certainly don't take away my grief. I will always mourn the lifetime together that we lost and the children we didn't get to see grow up, noting how one had his eyes and another had my nose. All that is gone. That earthly future with Trent is not to be. Yet he is here with me—not only in his name that I've made my own, but also in the lessons he taught me and his enduring encouragement and inspiration that have kept me going.

A few weeks after Trent died, I had been ready to say, "I'm done." I didn't know which way to turn anymore with my music, and I was ready to give it up. But now I believe Trent's destiny helped change my heart and show me that I have it within me to give God something greater. That's what I'm doing now, rejuvenating my music and sharing my testimony with audiences around the country, including the awesome Women of Faith conferences. I want to pay tribute to Trent and also show others, by his example, how they can become more thoughtful husbands and wives, more fun to be with, and how they can bring devotion to God into everything they do.

Before we'd left for Jamaica, I had applied for Trent to be a support runner in the Olympic Torch Relay, a sixty-five-day event in which runners would carry a torch across the United States to open the Olympics in Salt Lake City in early 2002. Fifteen days after Trent died, I was notified that his application had been accepted. The confirmation letter to Trent from Coca-Cola, the sponsoring organization, said, "You were nominated by your wife, Tammy, to be a 'guardian of the flame,' because you have inspired and touched Tammy's life every day, and she couldn't think of any other person more deserving to guard the flame."

I was allowed to run Trent's two-mile section in his place when the torch came through Nashville in December 2001. Trent's dad and sister Tara came down for the event, and my family came too. I woke up very early on the morning of the run to find a card lying on my bathroom counter. It simply said "TT" on the outside, and I could have sworn it was Trent's handwriting. I opened the card and read, "It's so hard not to be holding your hand right now, just when you need me the most. I can't think of a place I'd rather be than with you. But I can't change the circumstances. So, until I see you again, I'm sending you my heart filled with love and strength. Keep those thoughts close, as you are always in mine." It was signed, "Forever, Trent."

I sank to the floor, crying softly so I wouldn't wake up my house-guests (my family was staying with me for the event). The bathroom door gently opened, and Gina was standing there with tears falling from her face too. I knew at that moment that Gina had been the one who had bought that perfect card for me and left it in my bathroom, wanting me to know that Trent was still here with me, somehow, in that moment, that special day.

Ken drove me to the staging area early that morning (there was no need for the rest of the family to come hours before the event started). When we arrived, we learned that the organizers were short a runner. I asked if Ken could run too. I had asked him to run in Trent's place earlier, and he had told me, "Tammy, I would do anything for you, anything for Trent, but I think if anyone runs in his place, it should be you." Now, after a few phone calls, the officials decided we could both run. Once again, the Lord made sure I wasn't alone.

We called home and asked Gina to bring Ken's running shoes (the Olympic organizers gave all the runners sports outfits to wear, but we wore our own shoes). Ken ran his heart out, and as I handed him the torch, I thought, *How perfect this is. How Trent would have loved this!*

RELUCTANT CHANGES

The torch run was a bittersweet occasion, one I'll never forget. But when the excitement was over and my family went back home, I was left alone in my grief. The "big picture" of my life had changed enormously, and in response I fought to keep all the details the same. The fact was, at first I didn't want to change *anything*—didn't want to wash the sheets on our bed, didn't want to move Trent's yard shoes away from the kitchen door, didn't want to remove anything from his side of the closet. But gradually, bit by bit, I gave away some of his things to friends and family members.

While Dad Lenderink and Tara were in Nashville for the torch relay, I took Tara upstairs to the closet, and we filled the biggest box I could find with things that had been Trent's. It was hard for me to part with his belongings so soon after losing him, but I managed to do it, knowing that his things would have the same meaning for his family as they did for me.

As time passed, I gave away a few more pieces of Trent's clothes, but it was another year before I was able to move the things from beside his sink in the bathroom. I think I just kept waiting for him to come back and brush his teeth or use his shaver. Finally, piece by piece, I began moving things off the counter and putting them underneath the sink.

Then, a few months ago, I called a closet-organizing company to come redesign my closet. We worked together, and they made a drawing, following the needs I outlined—a long space for dresses, shorter space for skirts and slacks, racks for shoes, shelves for sweaters and such. Then, on the day they came to actually install the components, I had to empty the closet. I took out all the clothes and shoes—mine and Trent's—and laid them on the bed. When the workers were finished, they said, "OK, you can put your things away," and they left.

I began putting things back, arranging them in the specific places that had been created for them. I put everything in its place, and then I realized there was no longer a place for Trent's things. I sat there and cried, seeing this as another step toward living my life without him. I hung his clothes in a guestroom closet, crying the whole time, but also thanking God for helping me take that step.

I hadn't really thought about moving Trent's things from the closet when I called the organizer company. If I'd thought about it, I probably wouldn't have done it. I was just thinking I would make better use of the space. Then, when it was finished, it was as if God had planned it all to happen just as it did (which, of course, he did!). I sensed him saying to me, *I'll do this for you, Tammy. It's going to be hard, but the end result is what you need.*

FRUSTRATIONS

While I've managed to change a lot of things since I lost Trent, the little yellow note on the computer isn't one of them. It's still there—although it did disappear for a while.

Before Trent's death, I was terrible with computers, and although Trent tried to teach me, I refused to learn. Whenever I needed to write a letter to someone, he would have to bring up the software and open the document format, then I would sit down and begin to type. I can't count the times he said to me, "Baby, let me show you what to do. You just click here . . ."

But I would say, "No! Don't tell me. I don't want to know, Trent. I don't want to have too much information in my head. You can always just pull it up for me. You're always here, and when I need it, I'll ask you."

Sometimes Trent would smile and say, "Oh, Tammy Trent, you frustrate me."

After his death, I struggled to figure out anything at all on the computer. Late one night when I was trying for the first time to write a letter on my own, I sat at the computer and had no idea what to do. I started pushing keys and clicking on buttons and watching the screen change; I was getting nowhere. But that didn't stop me. I kept clicking and tapping and trying, and somehow I accidentally deleted that little sticky note from Trent.

Shocked by what I had done, I cried hysterically and kept pounding away at the keyboard and clicking away with the mouse, desperately trying to get it back. But it was gone. Finally I called Anita Rundell, my friend and webmaster, who knows everything about computers. I was crying so hard she could barely understand what the problem was.

She told me she would come over the next day and show me how to pull up a letter, and she said she would try to get the sticky note back. But I couldn't stand the thought of booting up the computer the next morning and not seeing Trent's note there. So I kept working at it and finally, late that night, I managed to get the little yellow square back on the screen. But now there were no words on it, so I kept working and working until I managed to retype Trent's words back on the note. I don't know how many hours I spent, urgently trying to get the note back. All I know is that now it's been almost three years since I lost Trent, and his note is still there.

"A TREASURE IN MY HEART"

Another thing I've kept in my life is my relationship with Dad and Mom Lenderink. In October 2003 they came to visit me, and although Mom had briefly seen the house just as construction ended in 1999 (but no decorating had been completed yet), that was the first time she and Dad had stayed in the home Trent and I had built.

We had a wonderful three days together, running around town, sharing memories through laughter and tears. I cooked for them, and they saw the woman I've become instead of the teenager who broke up with their son or acted immaturely.

I said my good-byes to them early on a Saturday morning because I had to catch a 6:00 a.m. flight. It felt a little awkward, leaving them alone and running off for a booking, but when I returned home two days later, I found a beautiful note on my kitchen counter. Mom Lenderink had written it, and Dad had added some notes here and there. Here's what it said.

Sat. 7:30 a.m.

Dear Tammy,

We had such a precious time with you. Although it brought many tears to my eyes and heart, our time together will be a treasure in my heart forever. You and Trent have built a beautiful home here, and Trent would be so proud of you for the additions you have added. [Here Dad jotted in the margin, "He told me of your many qualities—they are shining."]

Thank you for loving our son, not only in his life, but also in his death ["and new life," Dad wrote in the margin]. We love you deeply,

Dad & Mom #2

xxx ooo

[Here Dad wrote, "so blessed to see God's strength in Tammy Trent"

—Tom Dad "hug"]

P.S. [from Dad] We see more and more why he adored you so much! Smart guy he is.

18

New Life

Floating around to find my own ground,
Fell into you, this is when I knew
The flooding of rain, it's what made the change.
Now I can see all the colors in me.

Oh, I love your sun shining on me,
I can feel your wind blowing softly.
Can you see my spirit blooming?
New life has just begun in me.

Beauty will fall, oh, like nothing at all.
Standing in truth, it will carry me through.
When winter gives in, then I will begin
to spring up and say, What a beautiful day.

I'm coming to life again.
I'm coming to life again.
I'm learning to breathe again.

—Tammy Trent & Pete Orta

18 | on the road again

WHEN I CAME BACK FROM JAMAICA to Michigan, I had all kinds of dates on my book. Just a day or two after I got back, I picked up the phone and called every one of those bookings; I talked to the pastors or the organizers who had set up the dates. The conversation usually went something like this:

"Hello, this is Tammy Trent."

"Oh, Tammy! We're so sorry about Trent, and we're praying for you. What do you need? What can we do for you?"

"I don't need anything. I just wanted to tell you that I will be there next month [or in November, or whenever]. I'll be there; don't worry. I'll honor that contract; I'll come, and I will minister."

Then there would be a pause, and the person on the other end of the line would say, "Are you sure, Tammy? Are you sure you're ready?"

I would say, "Yes. I've never not shown up for a booking, and I just wanted to let you know that I'll be there."

Then a couple of days went by, and I absolutely fell apart. I looked at my mom and said, "What am I thinking? I can't do that show! I can't be there next month. I can barely walk across the bedroom floor; how can I climb up onto the stage again?"

Mom said gently, "Honey, I know. I know. Just do whatever you need to do. Call them back. They'll understand."

So I picked up the phone again and called every single one of them back. This time I said, "I'm so sorry, but I can't come. I just don't have the strength. I thought I could do it, but I can't."

And every single one of those pastors and organizers said, "Tammy, we totally understand." One pastor even said, "We couldn't believe you thought you *could* come. We couldn't imagine that you would be ready."

NOTHING TO GIVE

His words gave me something to think about. It dawned on me that there would probably be hundreds of other people who also would think, *We can't believe she's up there, not after what's just happened to her.* I realized that people who knew me would understand that I needed time to heal.

And there was something else. People often come to Christian concerts because they're searching. Sure, they come because they want to be entertained, but sometimes they come for other reasons too. They come because they're hurting, and they want relief from emotional or spiritual pain. They come because they don't know Jesus, and they want to—or they want to be inspired to know him better, to have a closer relationship with him. They come because they're looking for hope; they're looking for something to hang on to.

So when you're up on the platform, you feel like you need to have some answers for these people who've come to see you. And at that point, I felt like I had nothing to give them. I didn't have the answers for myself at that time, let alone for anyone else. I was struggling to understand why God had allowed Trent to be taken from me, and I couldn't bring myself to find any humor in my life. Plus I was very vulnerable during that time, very sensitive to criticism, and it seemed that the few times I did venture out into the public eye, I opened myself up to that.

In an e-mail I sent out to my mailing list, I admitted that I was afraid sometimes to come home to a dark, empty house. Right away, a couple of e-mails came back, saying things like, "Thou shalt not be afraid. Fear is not of the Lord!"

I got to a point where I felt I couldn't win, couldn't please everybody. There would be some people who would support how I felt and what I was going through, and others who would believe I was walking through grief all wrong. So I just withdrew from the spotlight and devoted myself to letting God heal me. I guess you might say I made a deal with him. I felt him telling me to come down off the platform, and I said, "OK, Jesus, give me a year, and after that year, I'm trusting you to show me what you want me to do with my life. Give me a year, then show me how I can serve you and glorify you in the next chapter of my life."

And that's what happened. I spent those months surrounding myself with people who loved me, and I focused on studying God's Word and listening more closely for his voice.

THE FIRST STEP BACK—INTO CHAOS

In late spring 2002, I got a call from my friend Greg Long, another Christian recording artist. He said, "Tammy, I don't know if you're ready, I don't know if you're feeling strong enough, but I'm going to do some dates in the fall, in September. Would you like to do a little tour with me?"

I told him I'd think about it and call him back. And as I considered his invitation, one fact kept rolling through my mind: *In September it will be one year since I lost Trent. One year exactly . . .*

The dates Greg mentioned were still more than four months away, but I couldn't imagine being ready to perform again then. Still, I knew I had to. *Well, here we go. Thank you, Jesus—doggone it! You do remember what we promise you!* I had had that conversation with the Lord, and I knew he was saying to me now, *Girl, you promised me; I promised you.*

So I called Greg back and said yes, I would go.

As the date drew near, I felt increasingly apprehensive about going back out on the road without Trent—and wondering if I still had what it takes to be a singer up there on the platform. For sure, I knew I couldn't travel alone. So I called Anita Rundell and asked if she would go with me. The first date was on a weekend in Peoria, Illinois; Greg would furnish us with transportation, and we would drive up to Peoria, do the concert, spend the night, and come home. Anita agreed to come along.

When the big day came, we piled into my car and drove over to

Franklin, Tennessee, where we were to load up the bus. Anita had never done anything like this, and I couldn't help feel a little smug, thinking, *This is going to be so cool for her. She's going to be so impressed. She'll probably be convinced I'm a rock star!* But when we pulled into the place where we were to meet the other guys, instead of a big, comfortable bus, we found a vehicle that resembled something a vagabond might live in down by the river! And as if the van wasn't bad enough, behind it was a huge boxlike wagon kind of thing that was bigger than the van and twice as scary looking!

Anita and I stood there looking at this unbelievable sight, and both of us were thinking the same thing: *Surely this is* not *our transportation.*

Nobody was around, and that was reassuring to me. I decided this rattletrap rig was actually the property of some homeless person, and our sleek, modern bus was probably running a little late and would come roaring in any minute.

Then I turned slightly and saw, walking toward us, a totally grunged-out guy with blue hair and black fingernails. The young man walking beside him was his total opposite, clean cut and "normal" looking. I looked at them, they looked at me, and then my heart stopped as one of them said, "Tammy Trent?"

My brain was silently screaming in terror, *Oh, dear Jesus, help us!* I was calculating whether I should grab Anita, jump back in my car, and peel out of the parking lot. But somehow, while these thoughts were zooming through my mind, I managed to smile slightly and nod my head.

I looked at Anita, embarrassed beyond words. Her face had a totally bewildered look, and I could tell that she was thinking, *Tammy, we're not getting in that van, are we?*

But yes, that's what we did. We crawled into the middle seat of the rickety old van and the two guys got in front, and off we went. As we got onto the Interstate, I admit that I didn't have the kindest thoughts toward Greg, who had flown on ahead to Peoria!

Now we're rumbling along the freeway, and—I kid you not—our *top speed* is fifty-five miles per hour. That's all the poor old van would do! But it was just as well, because the monstrous box we were towing was swaying all over the place, rocking the van from side to side as we rolled along.

At one point I looked at Anita, and she looked at me, and we obviously were having the identical thought: *We are going to die.*

And we weren't the only ones who were worried. As we struggled up the first big hill we had to cross, the guy who was driving shook his head and said, "I don't know if we're going to make it."

I pulled out my cell phone and said into it, as softly as I could, "Mom, you have to pray for us. We're in a van that's towing a thing the size of Montana, we're supposed to be at a concert *tonight* in Peoria, and it's gonna take a miracle for us to make it there."

By now Anita and I were laughing hysterically—but trying to hold it in, because, of course, we didn't want to hurt the guy's feelings. We knew he was doing the best he could. He was the sound engineer, and this was his first road trip. Now he was stuck driving this van, pulling this incredibly monstrous trailer, and all he needed was two hysterical women in the backseat.

Finally we calmed down and managed to doze off, lulled to sleep by the side-to-side swaying of the van and its mischievous "tail." Two hours into the drive, we were awakened by a big *bah-boom! bah-boom!* Then everything started slowing down—the swaying, the rumbling, the rolling along. I sat up and looked out the window. We were on the side of the road.

"What's happening?" I asked Mr. Blue Hair.

He sat there shaking his head for a moment. Then he turned around and told me, "We're out of gas."

All I could do was laugh. We're on our way to Peoria in a van built by Noah, and now we've run out of gas in the middle of nowhere. The two guys are on their cell phones, but since we don't know where we are, they're not much help. So they get out of the van and look this way and that, but there's not a single highway sign in sight. So they just start walking. (Anita is *really* impressed with what it means to be a Christian artist on tour!)

About an hour later they're back—empty-handed. They weren't able to find a gas station. So there we sat, wondering what on earth we were going to do. Finally one of the guys flagged down a man who agreed to take the two of them to the nearest gas station. Anita and I were a little concerned, wondering if we would ever see them again. But in another hour or so, back they came in a roadside-assistance truck. They had just enough gas to get us to the service station. We filled up and hit the road again.

The concert was fully booked—a packed house—and by the time we arrived in Peoria, everyone was rushing around frantically trying to get the sound and lighting set up, the backdrop rigged, and the merchandise tables prepared.

I was supposed to use Greg's band as my accompaniment, but I had also brought my performance tracks along, just in case they were needed—and they were. The sound system wasn't working, and Greg was saying when and if it got fixed there wouldn't be time for sound checks. Meanwhile, there were hundreds of people filling the lobby. The show was scheduled to start at 7:00, and it was now 7:30. And we still didn't have sound.

I was hurriedly trying to get my merchandise out and hoping to find a way to do a sound check. Meanwhile, poor Anita now was surely wondering what on earth I'd gotten her into! If she thought the van ride was awful, what must she be thinking now, when I had delivered her right into the heart of total chaos?

I took a moment to catch my breath and whisper a prayer. Then I told Anita, "Come with me. Come fast. I need you to go upstairs to the church's sound booth. Go up there, plug in my soundtracks. I'm going to have to use my sound tracks and not the band, and I *am* going to have a sound check, one way or another. Get the stage monitors, get me a microphone, and I will meet you on the stage."

Now hundreds of people were flowing into the auditorium. I got up on the platform just as the sound techs finally pulled up one of my tracks, and I tried my best to make things look like this was what we planned all along. "Hello! How's everybody tonight?" I said in between tests. "Thanks for coming to the show, and welcome to the sound check." I ran through a couple of tracks real quickly and left the stage.

BACK IN THE SPOTLIGHT

Despite the last-minute hitches, the concert was a success, and I felt blessed to be performing with Greg Long. He is a talented artist who truly loves the Lord, and he's like a brother to me. He didn't bring me along on this brief tour as his opening act; Greg opened the show himself. He sang for thirty minutes, then he stopped and introduced me, talking about my life and the tragedy that had occurred. He set the stage for my part of the program in a very sensitive way, and I came out and sang "Welcome Home" and shared my testimony.

I ran through my set list and ended with "My Irreplaceable." Then I walked off the stage, went back to the green room, and collapsed in relief, thinking, *I did it! I actually did it. I can do this. I'm grieving, but I'm going to make it.*

Since that first crazy time back on the stage, there have been a hundred others. God has helped me reclaim my ministry, and I am finding strength and hope in sharing my music again. While several things have made getting back on the platform difficult for me, the hardest of all is still looking out over the audience, back to the soundboard, and not seeing Trent standing back there. Seeing him there, pacing in the dimmed light of the auditorium, always grounded me, gave me confidence and security. Bringing him up on stage with me had become a highlight of any concert. But all that is in the past. I look back at the soundboard now and see the technician concentrating on his work. It's been nearly three years since I've stood on stage and heard Trent's voice whispering "I love you" in my ear monitor.

RELYING ON GOD

The truth is, I thought for a long time I just couldn't do it again without Trent, but God simply carried me through those first events until I understood that I *could* do it. I think he was showing me that I had relied too much on Trent and not enough on him. Losing Trent was part of God's plan, and, no surprise, I hated that part of it. But now, nearly three years later, I am convinced that it also was part of God's plan that I climb back up on the stage and continue a ministry in music.

The pressure has been intense. As a believer, a Christian artist is expected to have the right things to say—a strong testimony to share—and there's always going to be someone somewhere who is quick to criticize.

But God helped me persevere, even when I became frustrated that people misunderstood my feelings. Since that first short tour with Greg Long, I've resumed a full schedule and have been tremendously blessed by the opportunity to share my music and my message with the thousands of women who flock to the Women of Faith conferences around the country.

I've come back. But it has been a long, often difficult journey that has brought me to a new place in my life and in my career. When I returned from Jamaica, I booted up Trent's laptop and found nearly two thousand e-mails waiting for me! I've always been one who answers every single piece of fan mail—every note, every postcard, every e-mail—but at that point I was overwhelmed by the work ahead of me. Some of those who wrote simply expressed concern and love, and I could send off a quick thank you and be finished. But others wanted details: "How are you doing, Tammy? We're praying for you—what can we pray for?" Still others wanted to know *how* I was recovering from my grief: "Are you still walking with the Lord?" (Absolutely.) "Are you still wearing your wedding ring?" (Yes! I wear my own wedding ring on my left hand—and Trent's wedding band on my right. And I wear his watch.) "Did you take down Trent's pictures in your house?" (No, they're all still there, still providing poignant love and wonderful memories.)

Trent had always begged me to save my e-mails and build an e-mail address list, but as I'd done with so many of his technical suggestions, I'd ignored that one too. Now I realized how right he had been; I needed to be able to send out *one* e-mail to everyone who was writing to me. Fortunately, I had Anita, my friend and webmaster, who could help me build that list. Probably the smartest thing I did after that was to journal my recovery, recording the ups and downs of my life after losing Trent. It was awesome to see God use that process to heal me—and to reach out to others.

It also told me, early on, that I wasn't ready to go back on the platform yet because, for one thing, I was still feeling too vulnerable to criticism. The most hurtful e-mail I got in response to those journaling e-mails came from a pastor I didn't know but who had ended up on my e-mail list. He accused me of idolizing Trent's memory and told me that, after three months, it was "time to move on." He added that there was probably some man in the world right now who would be willing to marry me, travel with me, and minister alongside of me.

Stung by his words, I clicked on the REPLY button way too fast and wrote, "You don't know me, you don't know my heart, and you didn't know Trent. How could you possibly know what God wants for me?" I must admit, I sort of felt sorry for that pastor's church!

STILL RANTING AND RAVING . . . BUT BREATHING AGAIN

While I occasionally let my temper show around a family member or close friend during this grieving process, I really never got angry with God. I never shook my fist at him and ranted, "This is your fault! Why did you take him from me? I hate this. I hate you!" I've never done that, but I vented in other ways. Heaven help the inanimate objects that have been less than cooperative with me during this time!

For example, I spent four hundred dollars on a new case for my concert backdrop, and when it arrived, it was the wrong size—but I didn't know that when I tried to put the backdrop in the new case. So I spent a long time in the foyer of my house wrestling with the case and the backdrop. I was shoving it and turning it and jerking it this way and that, and it wouldn't go in, and I finally threw the case across the floor and yelled, "I hate this! I hate all this. I hate having to be strong all the time, and I've gotta get up on that platform talking about how good God is, and if you're so good, God, then why can't you just help me with this stupid case?"

I kicked the case and broke a piece off it, then I went into the office, still boiling, and in my anger I swung my arm and knocked a plate of potpourri off the cabinet. Just *wham!* and it flew off.

Anita happened to be there, and it was her first glimpse of a full-fledged Tammy Trent temper tantrum. She was shocked. I ran upstairs and lay on my bed, sobbing, for the longest time. And then it was over, and of course I felt awful about it, embarrassed, guilty, and ashamed that my dear friend had seen that ugly side of me. But, just as Trent had done, Anita let me vent and left me alone for a while, then she tiptoed up the stairs, tapped at the door, and asked, "Tammy, are you OK? Do you need anything?"

Well, yes, I did need something. I needed to apologize! "Please forgive me, Anita," I said.

The lawn mower has also become a target of my wrath (but deservedly so, if you ask me!). Trent always mowed our yard, and since he died, I've been doing it myself. But the darn mower seems to have a mind of its own, and right on the steep part of our sloping backyard, it suddenly quits and refuses to be started again, and, oh my goodness! The frustration I feel.

At one point last summer, the mower pulled this trick for what seemed like the ten-thousandth time, and after I had yanked and yanked and yanked on that cord, and the mower still wouldn't start, I just plopped down in the grass and started to cry.

"God, can't you just help me here?" I whined. "I've made it through the biggest test of all, and now I need you to help me in the little things. You're supposed to be there for the widow; everybody says that—you said so yourself. I hate that I'm a widow, but you're supposed to be there for the orphans and the widows, so can you just *be here* and help me start the stupid lawnmower? All I want . . ." I pulled it again, and it wouldn't start. "See!? You're not even listening to me! No one is listening to me."

I sat there and cried awhile, then I pushed the mower onto a flat surface and yanked it and yanked it—still crying—and it started. I stuck out my jaw and said, "That's better. OK. Here I go." And off I went to finish the lawn.

The lawnmower and I have tangled several times. Once I stood there in the backyard screaming at it. "I'm getting' tired of all this!" I exploded. "This sucks! I hate my whole life right now!" I yanked the cord again, and the beast just sputtered at me without starting. And then that awful word exploded out of my mouth. I'm not one who curses, and I didn't grow up in a family that swore; Trent never swore either. But out there on the lawn with that uncooperative lawn mower, I hissed out the S word, and I'll admit, it felt good. So I said it again: "S—!"

That night I was mortified by the memory of what I'd said and hoped with all my heart that my neighbors hadn't heard my explosion. I called my mom and confessed what I'd done. She said, "Honey, sometimes we do things we don't like. All of us do, and you know what? God can handle it. He can *so* handle it. Don't ever think he can't."

I'm embarrassed, picturing God looking down from heaven, laughing at my outburst, and saying, *That's really stupid, Tammy, but I can take it. I'm still here; I'm not going anywhere.*

Through everything that's happened—the grief, the hurt, the confusion, the anger—he has proven that to me again and again. He's still here. He's not going anywhere. Those thoughts have been the result of how I trust him, how I cling to him, how I depend on him for everything I do. If I could have a conversation with Trent right now, I think he would be the first to point that out to me. I can hear him say, *Girl, you're doing exactly what you're supposed to do. I had to go away, but God is using your grief for something very powerful. Don't give up, Tammy. You're gonna be just fine. I'm so proud of you!*

My heart still hurts, and even though I've lost Trent, I'm feeling more complete with each passing season. That kind of strength can only come from God. He is truly filling the void, and I find myself in the amazing situation of having a heart that's still broken but a life that's once again becoming full. I will always miss Trent, but I'm learning to be happy again, realizing God remains forever constant in my life. It's still a fight some days, but I'm choosing life. I'm choosing peace. I'm choosing joy.

God remains forever constant. That's the one thing that's kept me going, and it's the most important thing I share with audiences around the country. No matter what, God's still here, and at the end of the day, God is enough. Always has been, always will be. He can handle whatever we dish out. He laughs with us in the good times, he carries us through the pain, and when tragedy knocks the wind out of us, he helps us learn to breathe again.

credits

Chapter 1

"Jehovah Jira" by Merve and Merla Watson. © 1974 Catacomb Publishing. Used by permission.

Chapter 3

"He's Right There" by Lisa Kimmey Bragg and Todd Collins. © 2000 Gotee Music/BMI/Admin. by EMI Christian Music Publishing. All Rights Reserved. Copyright Secured. Used By Permission.

Chapter 4

"My Father's Eyes" by Gary Chapman. © 1978 Paragon Music Corporation/New Spring Publishing Inc./ASCAP. All Rights Reserved. Copyright Secured. Used By Permission.

"Giggle" by Amy Grant. © 1979 Word Music, LLC. All Rights Reserved. Used By Permission.

Our Vision

To see women set free to a lifestyle of God's grace.

Our Mission

To host events and create resources that nurture women spiritually, emotionally, and in their relationships with others.

Our Core Values

- The transforming power of grace
- Striving for excellence
- Honoring God and His people
- The power of story and the healing of humor
- Modeling community
- Living in faith

Our Audience

Women of Faith is communicating God's unconditional love regardless of religious affiliation.

For more information call **1-888-49-FAITH** or visit **womenoffaith.com**

WOMEN OF FAITH
A Division of Thomas Nelson, Inc.

PRESENTS

Irrepressible
HOPE
C O N F E R E N C E   2 0 0 4

Tammy Trent
Popular recording artist with a heart-rending story of tragedy and hope. Tammy will be appearing with Women of Faith at the cities highlighted below.

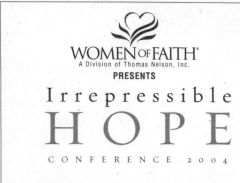

Featured Speakers & Dramatist:

Patsy Clairmont

Nicole Johnson

Marilyn Meberg

Luci Swindoll

Sheila Walsh

Thelma Wells

There is more to life than just staying afloat!
Experience the all-new two day conference that can put fresh wind in your sails — with stirring music, engaging dramatic presentations and refreshing messages.

We have this hope as an anchor for the soul, firm and secure.
—HEBREWS 6:19

2004 Event Cities & Dates*

Shreveport, LA
February 27-28
CenturyTel Center

Philadelphia, PA - I
March 5-6
Wachovia Spectrum

San Antonio, TX
March 18-20
AlamoDome

Ft. Wayne, IN
March 26-27
Allen County
War Memorial
Coliseum

Spokane, WA
April 16-17
Spokane Arena

Cincinnati, OH
April 23-24
US Bank Arena

San Jose, CA
May 7-8
HP Pavilion

Nashville, TN
May 14-15
Gaylord Entertainment
Center

Charleston, SC
May 21-22
N. Charleston Coliseum

Des Moines, IA
June 4-5
Veterans Memorial
Auditorium

Anaheim, CA - I
June 18-19
Arrowhead Pond

Pittsburgh, PA
June 25-26
Mellon Arena

Denver, CO
July 9-10
Pepsi Center

Ft. Lauderdale, FL
July 16-17
Office Depot Center

St. Louis, MO
July 23-24
Savvis Center

Atlanta, GA
July 30-31
Philips Arena

Washington, DC
August 6-7
MCI Center

Buffalo, NY
August 13-14
HSBC Arena

Ohama, NE
August 20-21
Qwest Center Omaha

Dallas, TX
August 27-28
American Airlines Center

Anaheim, CA - II
September 10-11
Arrowhead Pond

Albany, NY
September 17-18
Pepsi Arena

Philadelphia, PA - II
September 24-25
Wachovia Center

Hartford, CT
October 1-2
Hartford Civic Center

Portland, OR
October 8-9
Rose Garden Arena

Orlando, FL
October 15-16
TD Waterhouse Centre

St. Paul, MN
October 22-23
Xcel Energy Center

Charlotte, NC
October 29-30
Charlotte Coliseum

Oklahoma City, OK
November 5-6
Ford Center

Vancouver, BC
November 12-13
GM Place

*Dates, locations and special guests subject to change. **Special National Conference. Call 1-888-49-FAITH for details.

For more information call **1-888-49-FAITH** or visit **womenoffaith.com**

WOMEN OF FAITH®
A Division of Thomas Nelson, Inc.

PRESENTS

Tammy Trent
Women of Faith is delighted to annouce that Tammy Trent will join us in 2005 for Extraordinary Faith in selected cities.

EXTRAORDINARY FAITH
C O N F E R E N C E   2 0 0 5

Featured Speakers & Dramatist:
Patsy Clairmont, Nicole Johnson, Marilyn Meberg, Luci Swindoll , Sheila Walsh and Thelma Wells

New messages, new drama, new music, new special guests — with the same laughter and heart-felt emotions you've come to expect at a Women of Faith event.

Faith teaches us to trust when we don't have all the answers.

> *"Faith means being sure of the things we hope for. And faith means knowing something is real even if we do not see it."*
> *— Hebrews 11:1 (ncv)*

2005 Event Cities & Dates*

Ft. Lauderdale, FL¨
February 24-26
Office Depot Center

Shreveport, LA
April 1-2
CenturyTel Center

Houston, TX
April 8-9
Toyota Center

Columbus, OH
April 15-16
Nationwide Arena

Glendale, AZ (Phoenix)
April 22-23
Glendale Arena

Billings, MT
May 13-14
MetraPark

Pittsburgh, PA
May 20-21
Mellon Arena

Kansas City, KA
June 3-4
Kemper Arena

Buffalo, NY
June 10-11
HSBC Arena

St. Louis, MO
June 17-18
Savvis Center

East Rutherford, NJ
June 24-25
Continental Airlines Arena

Canada & New England
Cruise
June 25-July 2

Atlanta, GA
July 8-9
Philips Arena

Ft. Wayne, IN
July 15-16
Allen County War
Memorial Col.

Detroit , MI
July 22-23
Palace of Auburn Hills

Washington, DC
July 29-30
MCI Center

Sacramento , CA
August 5-6
Arco Arena

Portland , OR
August 12-13
Rose Garden Arena

Denver, CO
August 19-20
Pepsi Center

Dallas, TX
August 26-27
American Airlines Center

Anaheim, CA
September 9-10
Arrowhead Pond

Philadelphia, PA
September 16-17
Wachovia Center

Albany, NY
September 23-24
Pepsi Arena

Hartford, CT
Sept. 30 – October 1
Hartford Civic Center

Seattle, WA
October 7-8
Key Arena

Des Moines, IA
October 14-15
Wells Fargo Arena

St. Paul, MN
October 21-22
Xcel Energy Center

Charlotte, NC
October 28-29
Charlotte Coliseum

Oklahoma City, OK
November 4-5
Ford Center

Orlando, FL
November 11-12
TD Waterhouse Centre

Dates, locations and special guests subject to change. ¨Special National Conference. Call 1-888-49-FAITH for details.

For more information call **1-888-49-FAITH** or visit **womenoffaith.com**